ESTATE PUBL

SHROPSHIRE

Street maps with index
Administrative Districts
Population Gazetteer
Road Map with index
Postcodes

COUNTY RED BOOKS

This atlas is intended for those requiring street maps of the historical and commercial centres of towns within the county. Each locality is normally presented on one or two pages and although, with many small towns, this space is sufficient to portray the whole urban area, the maps of large towns and cities are for centres only and are not intended to be comprehensive. Such coverage in Super and Local Red Books (see page 2).

Every effort has been made to verify the accuracy of information in this book but the publishers cannot accept responsibility for expense or loss caused by any error or omission. Information that will be of assistance to the user of these maps will be welcomed.

The representation of a road, track or footpath on the maps in this atlas is no evidence of the existence of a right of way.

Street plans prepared and published by ESTATE PUBLICATIONS, Bridewell House, TENTERDEN, KENT.
The Publishers acknowledge the co-operation of the local authorities
of towns represented in this atlas.

Ordnance Survey® This product includes mapping data licensed from Ordnance Survey®
with the permission of the Controller of Her Majesty's Stationery Office.

COUNTY RED BOOK

SHROPSHIRE

contains street maps for each town centre

SUPER & LOCAL RED BOOKS

are street atlases with comprehensive local coverage

SHREWSBURY

including: Bayston Hill, Bicton Heath, Bomere Heath,
Harlescott, Shawbury etc.

TELFORD

including: Admaston, Dawley, Ironbridge, Madeley,
Oakengates, Wellington etc.

CONTENTS

LEGEND TO STREET MAPS

One-Way Street	→	Post Office	●
Pedestrianized		Public Convenience	C
Car Park	P	Place of Worship	+

Scale of street plans: 4 Inches to 1 mile (unless otherwise stated on the map).

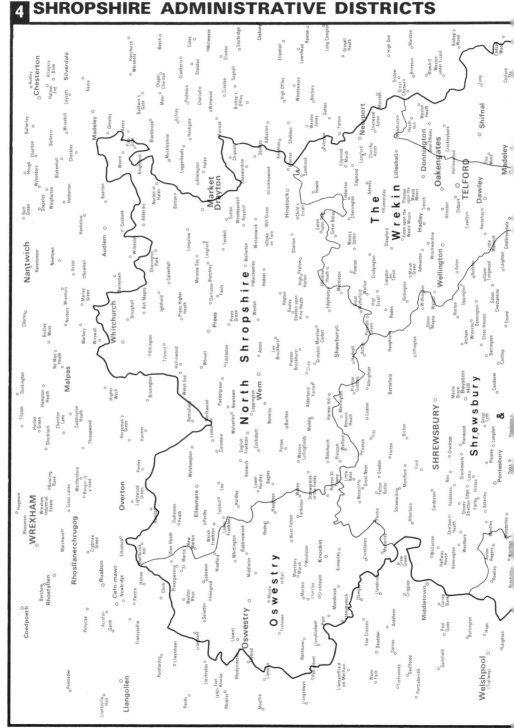

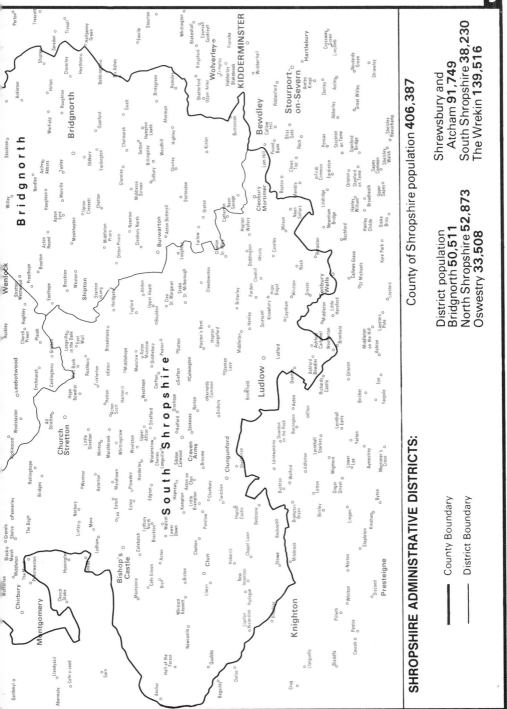

SHROPSHIRE ADMINISTRATIVE DISTRICTS:

County of Shropshire population **406,387**

District population
Bridgnorth **50,511**
North Shropshire **52,873**
Oswestry **33,508**

Shrewsbury and
Atcham **91,749**
South Shropshire **38,230**
The Wrekin **139,516**

—— County Boundary

—— District Boundary

5

GAZETTEER INDEX TO ROAD MAP

with Populations   County of Shropshire population 406,387

Place	Pop.	Grid
...ighton &		
...Eaton Constantine	433	11 F2
...leshall &		
...Donnington	10,810	9 G4
...ley		10 C3
...tle Brampton		10 C5
...tle Ness	199	8 C4
...tle Stretton		10 D3
...tle Wenlock	514	9 F5
...anfair Waterdine	192	10 A5
...anyblodwel	851	8 A3
...anymynech &		
Pant	1,393	8 B4
...awnt		8 B3
...wyn		10 B5
...ynclys		8 B3
...ckleywood		9 G3
...ngden	1,143	10 D2
...ngdon upon Tern		9 F4
...ngford (Market Drayton)		9 F2
...ngford (Newport)		9 G4
...ngnor	266	10 D2
...ngslow		9 F2
...ngville in the Dale		11 E3
...pington	495	8 D3
...ughton		11 F4
...wer Down		10 C4
...wer Frankton		8 C2
...wer Hordley		8 C3
...dford	384	11 E6
...dlow	9,011	11 E5
...dbury North	558	10 C4
...dham	211	10 C3
...neal		8 D2
...adeley	17,909	11 G2
...aesbrook		8 B4
...aesbury Marsh		8 B3
...ainstone	111	10 B4
...archamley		9 F3
...arket Drayton	9,482	9 F2
...arshbrook		10 D4
...arsh Green		9 F5
...arton		10 B2
...eadowtown		10 B2
...elverley	135	8 B4
...eole Brace		8 D5
...errington		8 D4
...iddlehope		10 D4
...iddleton (Chirbury)		10 B2
...iddleton (Ludlow)		11 E5
...iddleton (Oswestry)		8 B3
...iddleton Priors		11 F4
...iddleton Scriven	69	11 F4
...ill Green		9 F3
...ilson	99	11 F6
...insterley	1,397	10 C2
...inton		10 D3
...onkhopton	186	11 F3
...ontford	451	8 C5
...orda		8 B3
...ore	112	10 C3
...oreton Corbet &		
Lee Brockhurst	323	9 E3
...oreton Say	481	9 F2
...orton		8 B3
...orville	320	11 F3
...uch Wenlock	2,585	11 F2
...uckleton		9 E4
...unslow	405	11 E4
...yddle &		
Broughton	1,200	8 D3
...yndtown	78	10 C4
...antmawr		8 B3
...ash		11 F6
...een Savage	301	11 F5
...eed Sollars	138	11 F6
Neenton	121	11 F4
Nesscliffe		8 C4
Newcastle on Clun	264	10 B5
New Invention		10 B5
New Marton		8 C2
Newport	9,664	9 G4
Newtown		8 D2
Noneley		8 D3
Norbury	121	10 C3
Nordley		11 G3
Northwood		8 D2
Norton (Craven Arms)		10 D5
Norton (Madeley)		11 G2
Norton (Wellington)		9 E5
Norton in Hales	530	9 G2
Nox		8 C5
Oakengates	8,380	
(Telford)		9 G5
Oaks		10 D2
Oldbury		11 G3
Oldpark		9 F5
Ollerton		9 F3
Onibury	307	10 D5
Oreton		11 F5
Oswestry	14,219	8 B3
Oswestry Rural	3,497	*
Overdale & Lawley	3,990	9F5
Overton		10 D6
Paddolgreen		8 D2
Pant & Llanmynech	1,393	8 B2
Peaton		11 E4
Pennerley		10 C2
Pentre		8 C4
Peplow		9 F3
Perthy		8 C2
Petton	68	8 D3
Picklescott		10 D2
Pimhill	1,981	*
Pipe Gate		9 G1
Pitchford	99	11 E2
Plaish		11 E3
Plealey		8 D6
Plowden		10 C4
Ploxgreen		10 C2
Pontesbury	2,875	10 C2
Poynton Green		9 E4
Prees	2,713	9 E2
Prees Green		9 E2
Preesgweene		8 B2
Prees Higher Heath		9 E2
Prescott		8 D4
Presthope		11 E3
Preston Brockhurst		9 E3
Preston Gubbals		8 D4
Preston upon the		
Weald Moors	219	9 F4
Priestweston		10 B3
Priorslee &		
St Georges	6,578	*
Puleston		9 G4
Pulverbatch		10 D2
Purloque		10 B5
Purslow		10 C5
Quabbs		10 A5
Quatford		11 G3
Quatt		11 G4
Quatt Malvern	228	*
Randlay &		
Hollinswood	6,628	9 G5
Ratlinghope	134	10 C3
Rednal		8 C3
Richard's Castle	287	10 D6
Roden		9 E4
Rodington	778	9 E5
Romsley	133	11 H4
Rorrington		10 B2
Rosehill		9 F3
Roughton		11 G3
Rowley		8 B6
Rowton		9 F4
Ruckley & Langley	62	11 E2
Rudge	85	*
Rushbury	501	11 E3
Rushton		9 F5
Ruyton-XI-Towns	836	8 C4
Ryton	130	11 G2
St Georges &		
Priorslee	6,578	*
St Martins	2,513	8 B2
Sambrook		9 G3
Selattyn and		
Gobowen	3,357	8 B2
Shavington Park		9 F2
Shawbury	2,457	9 E4
Sheinton	78	11 F2
Shelderton		10 C5
Shellbrook Hill		8 C1
Shelve with		
Worthen	1,955	10 C2
Sherrifhales	648	9 G5
Shifnal	6,516	9 G5
Shipley		11 H3
Shipton	119	11 E3
Shrawardine		8 C4
Shrewsbury	64,440	8 D5
Sibdon Carwood	85	10 C4
Sidbury	44	11 G4
Siefton		10 D4
Sleapford		9 F4
Smethcott	182	*
Snailbeach		10 C2
Snitton		11 E5
Soudley		9 G3
Stanton Lacy	325	10 D5
Stanton Long	182	11 E4
Stanton upon		
Hine Heath	480	9 E3
Stanwardine in the Fields		8 C3
Stapleton		10 D2
Stirchley &		
Brookside	10,462	*
Stockton	317	11 G2
Stoke upon Tern	1,500	9 F3
Stoke St Milborough		11 E5
Stokesay	2,284	10 D5
Stoney Stretton		8 C5
Stottesdon	589	11 F3
Stowe	121	10 B6
Strefford		10 D4
Stretton Heath		8 C5
Stretton Westwood		11 E3
Sutton (Bridgnorth)		11 G4
Sutton (Ludlow)		11 E4
Sutton upon Tern	1,234	9 F2
Sutton Maddock	258	11 G2
Tasley	368	11 G3
Telford	122,191	9 G5
Ternhill		9 F2
Tetchill		8 C2
The Bog		10 C3
The Gorge	2,583	*
The Wyke		9 G5
Tibberton &		
Cherrington	650	9 G4
Ticklerton		10 D3
Tilstock		9 E2
Tong	249	9 H5
Trefonen		8 B3
Trench & Wrockwardine		
Wood	4,829	9 F5
Tugford		11 E4
Twichen		10 C5
Uffington	196	9 E5
Upper Affcot		10 D4
Upper Heath		11 E4
Upper Longwood		9 F5
Uppington &		
Wroxeter	393	9 E5
Upton Cressett	35	11 F3
Upton Magna	345	9 E5
Vennington		8 C5
Vernolds Common		10 D5
Walcot (Bishops Castle)		10 C4
Walcot (Wellington)		9 E5
Walford		8 D4
Wall Bank		10 D3
Walton		9 E4
Waters Upton	837	9 F4
Wellington	17,747	
(Telford)		9 F5
Welshampton &		
Lyneal	784	8 D2
Welsh End		9 E2
Welsh Frankton		8 C2
Wem Rural	1,472	*
Wem Urban	4,882	8 D3
Wentnor	208	10 C3
Westbury	1,110	8 C5
West Felton	945	8 C3
Westhope		10 D4
Westley		8 C5
Weston		11 F3
Weston Heath		9 H5
Weston Lullingfields		8 D3
Weston Rhyn	2,287	8 B2
Weston-under-		
Redcastle	247	9 E3
Wheathill	174	*
Whitchurch Rural	1,454	*
Whitchurch Urban	7,868	9 E1
Whitcott Keysett		10 B4
Whittingslow		10 D4
Whitton	91	11 E6
Whixall	803	9 E2
Willey		11 F2
Wistanstow	696	10 D4
Wistanswick		9 F3
Withington	220	9 E5
Wollaston	219	8 B5
Wollerton		9 F3
Wolverley		8 D2
Woodcote &		
Chetwynd Aston	463	9 G4
Woodhill		11 G4
Woodseaves		9 G3
Woolstaston	61	10 D3
Woolston		
(Church Stretton)		10 D4
Woolston (Oswestry)		8 B3
Woore	1,076	9 G1
Worfield	1,966	11 G3
Worthen with		
Shelve	1,955	10 B2
Worthertan		10 B2
Wrockwardine	2,246	9 F5
Wrockwardine Wood &		
Trench	4,829	9 F5
Wroxeter &		
Uppington	393	9 E5
Wyke		11 F2
Wykey		8 C3
Yeaton		8 D4
Yockleton		8 C5
Yorton		8 D3

...opulation figures (in bold type) are based upon the 1991 census and relate to the local authority area or parish as constituted at that date. Boundaries of the ...stricts are shown on pages 4-5. Places with no population figure form part of a larger local authority area or parish.

*Place not included on map due to limitation of space

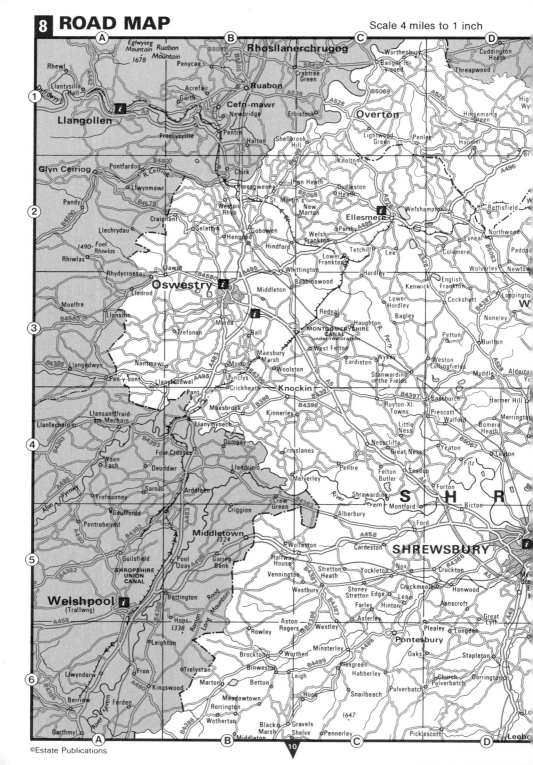

©Estate Publications

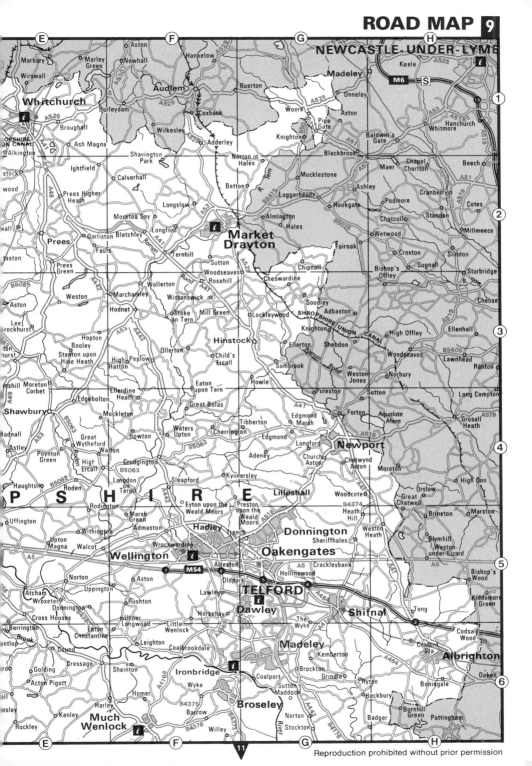

NEWCASTLE-UNDER-LYME

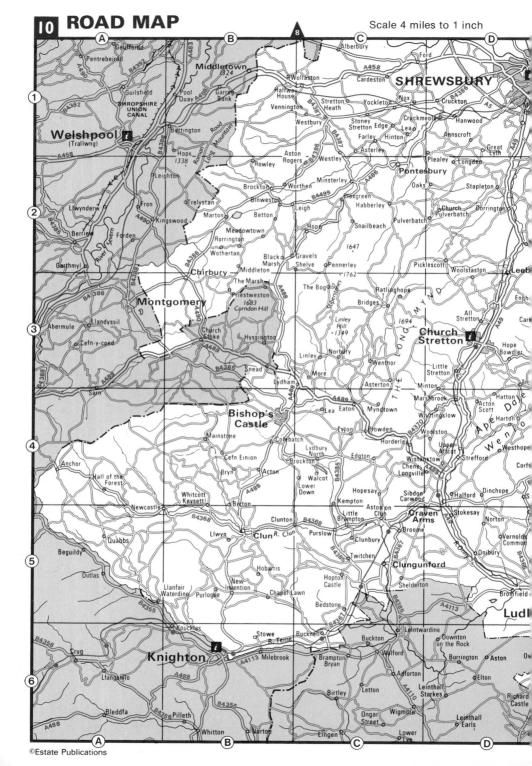

ROAD MAP

10

Scale 4 miles to 1 inch

©Estate Publications

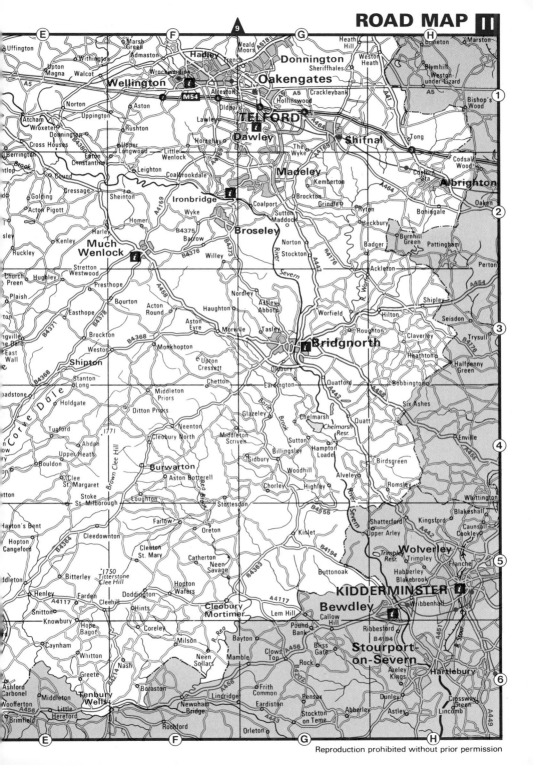

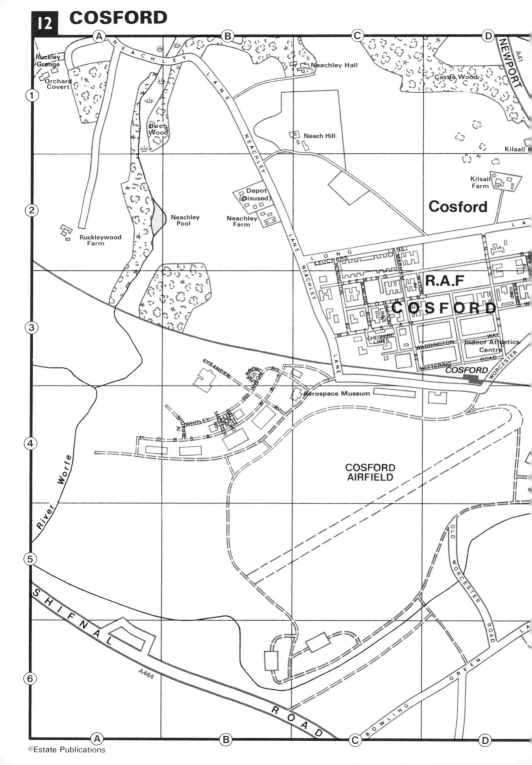

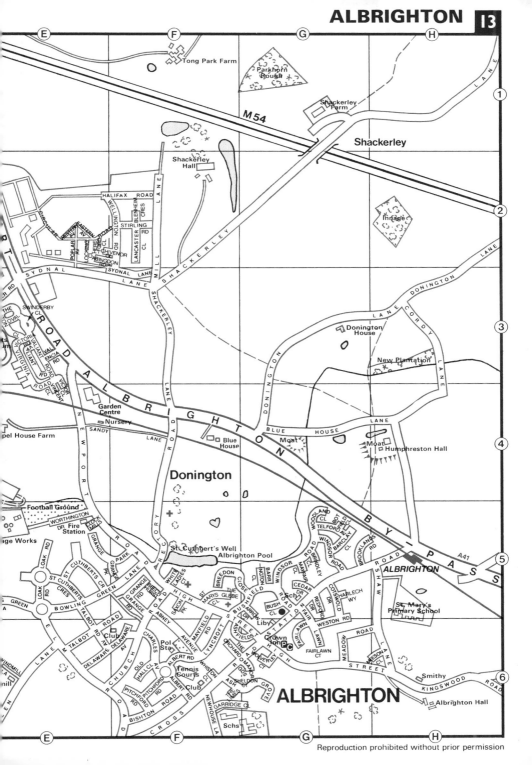

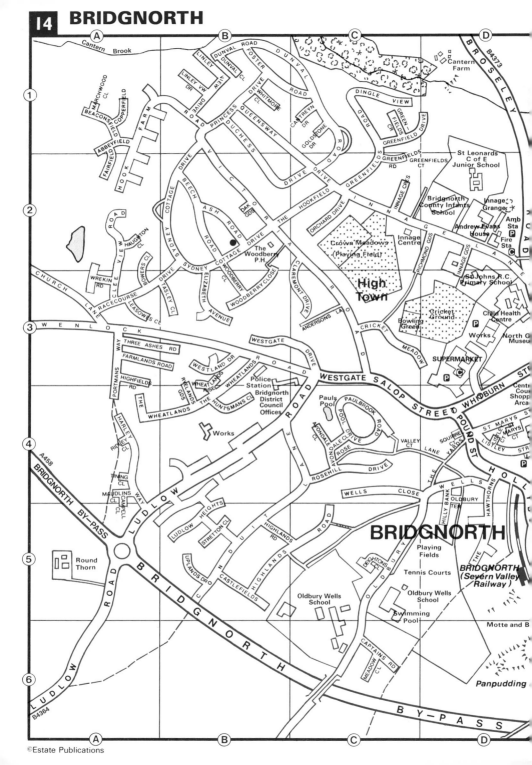

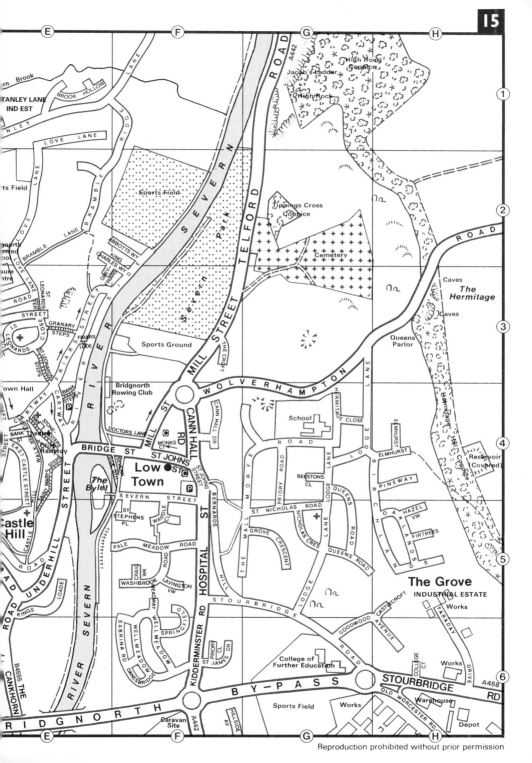

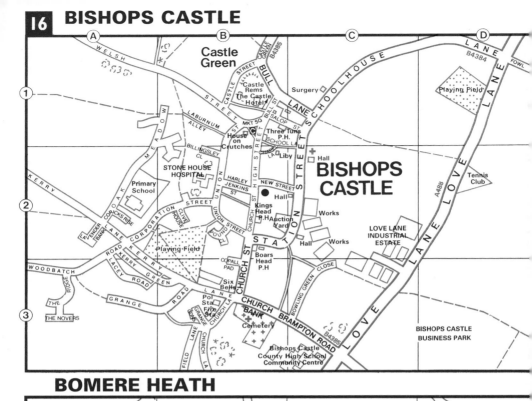

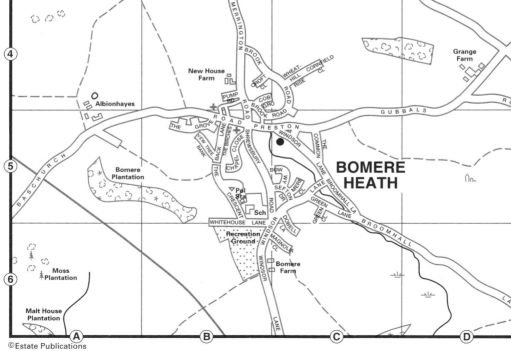

BOMERE HEATH

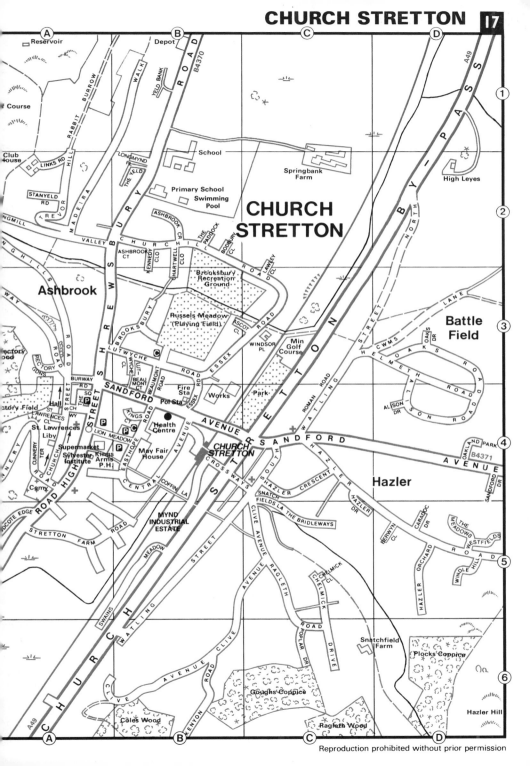

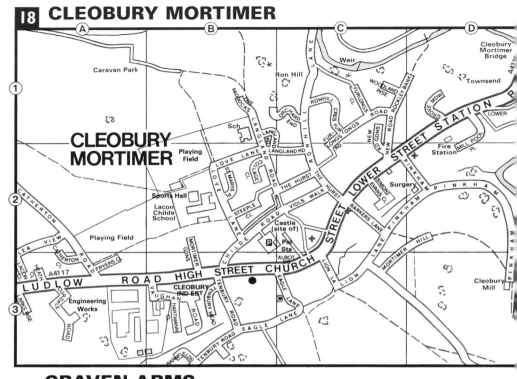

CRAVEN ARMS

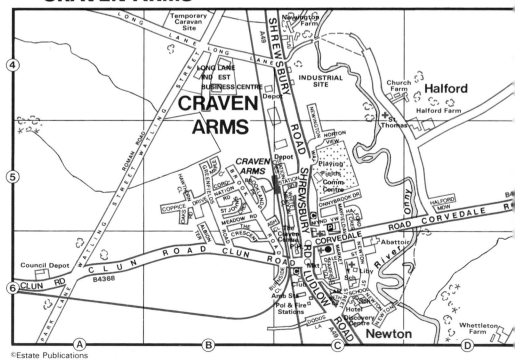

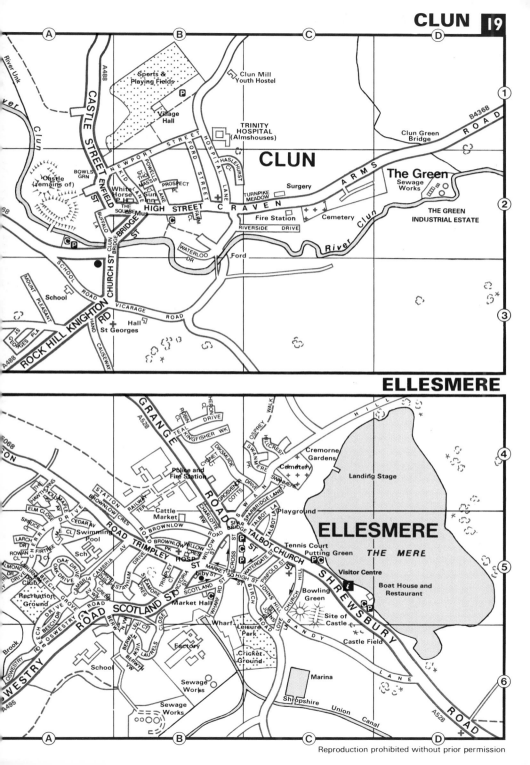

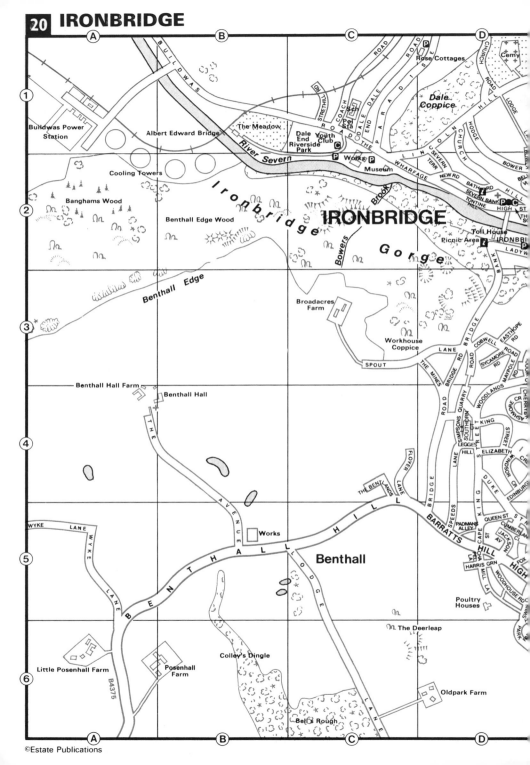

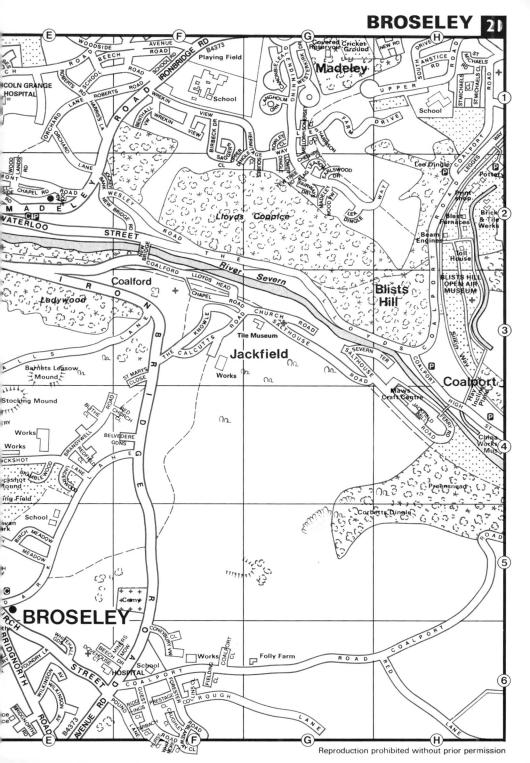

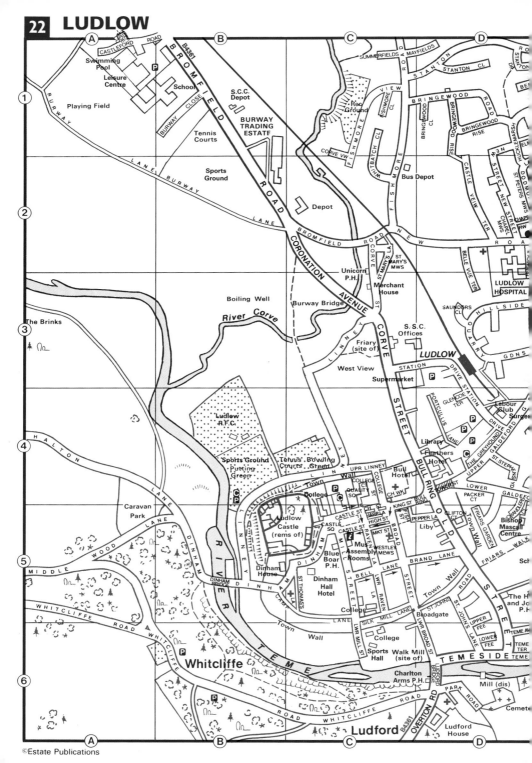

23

LUDLOW

Rocks Green

Reproduction prohibited without prior permission

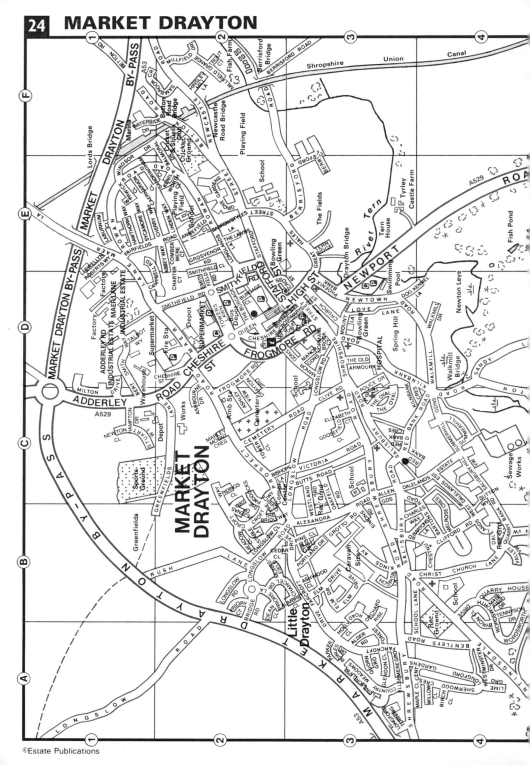

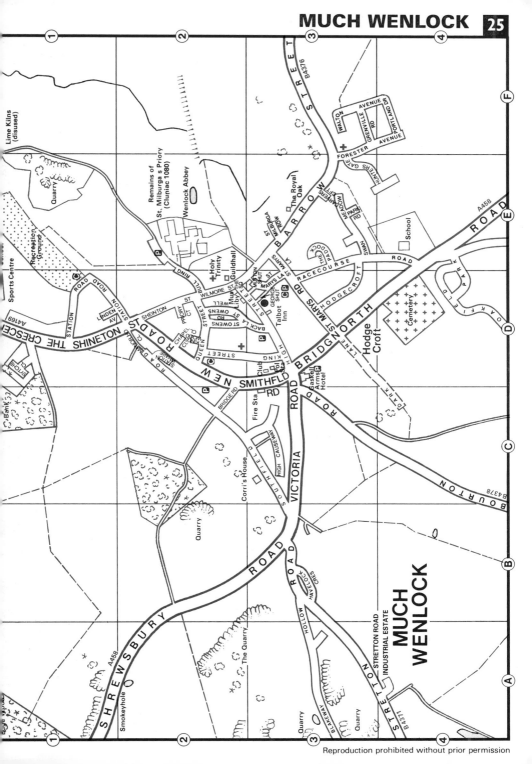

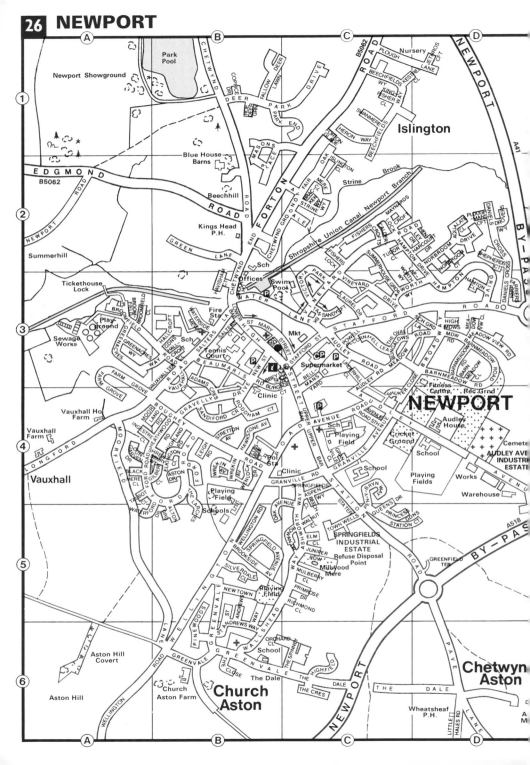

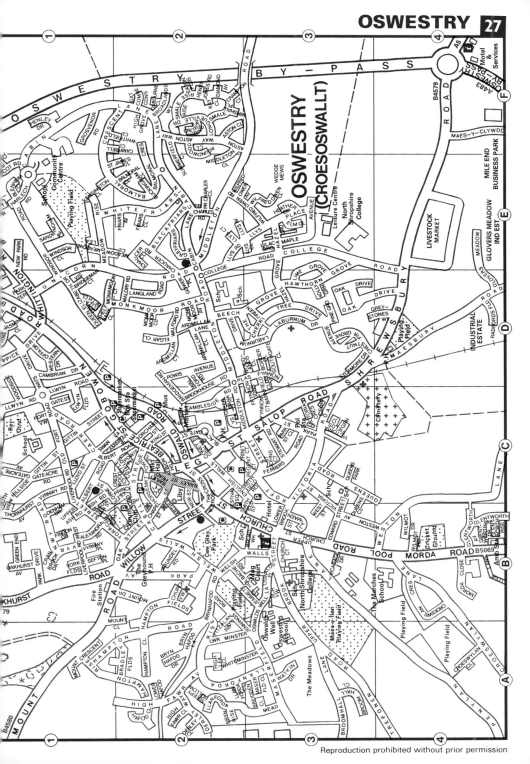

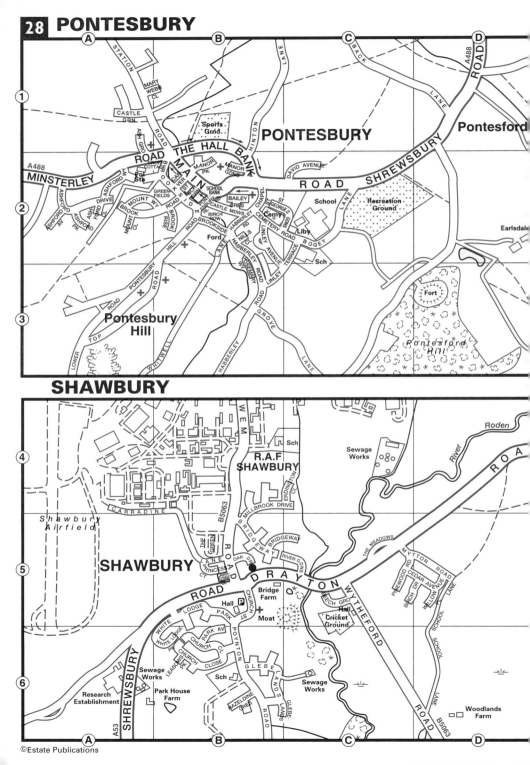

28 PONTESBURY

SHAWBURY

©Estate Publications

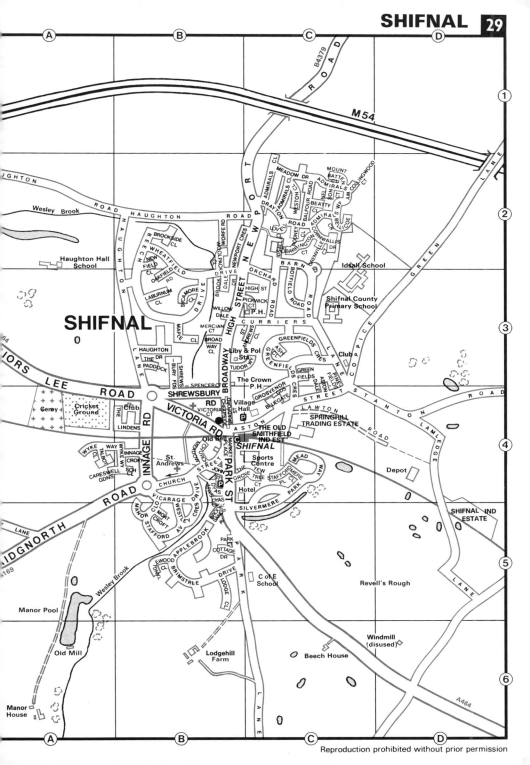

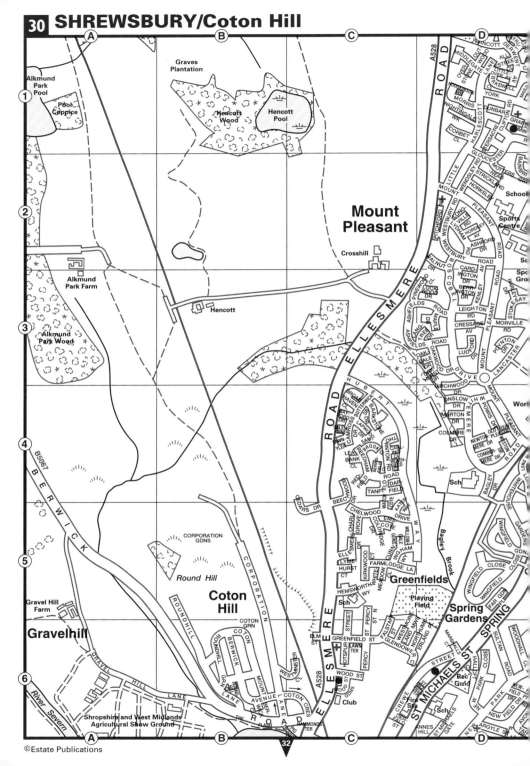

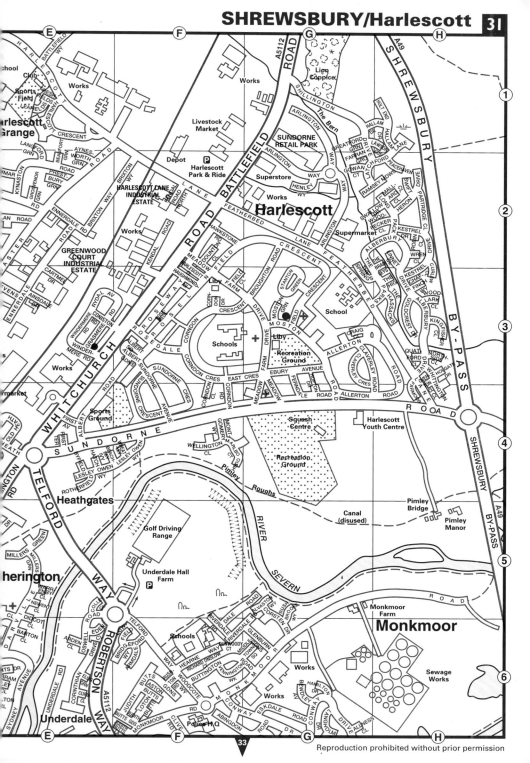

Harlescott

Heathgates

Monkmoor

Underdale

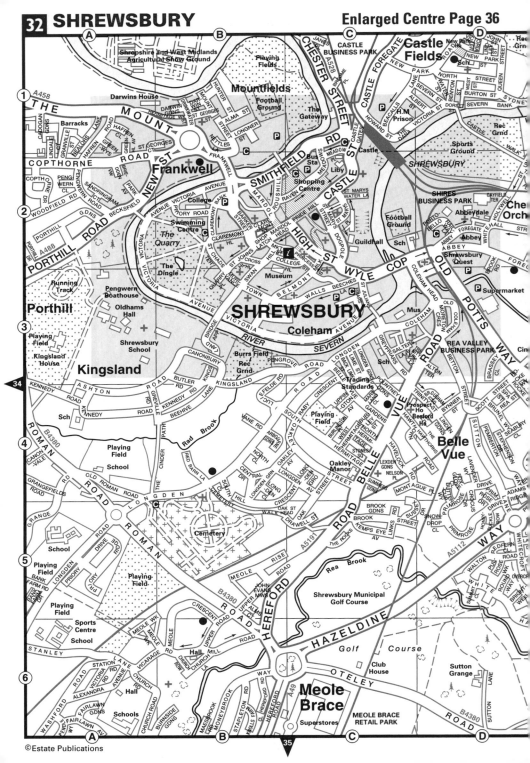

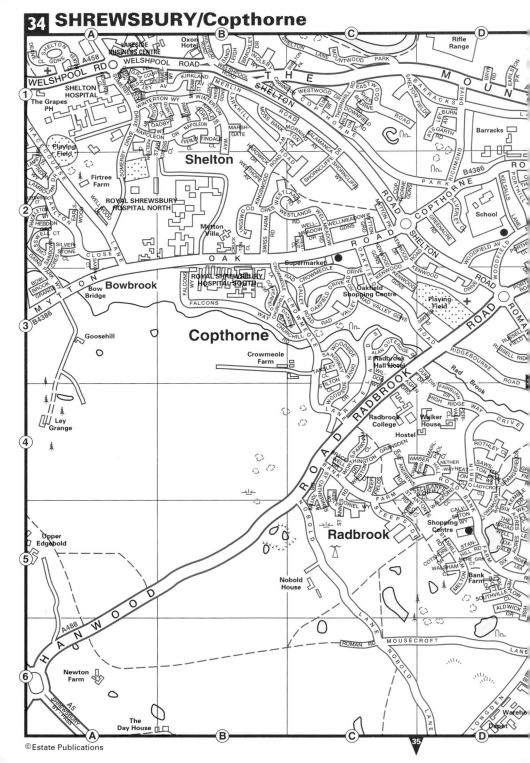

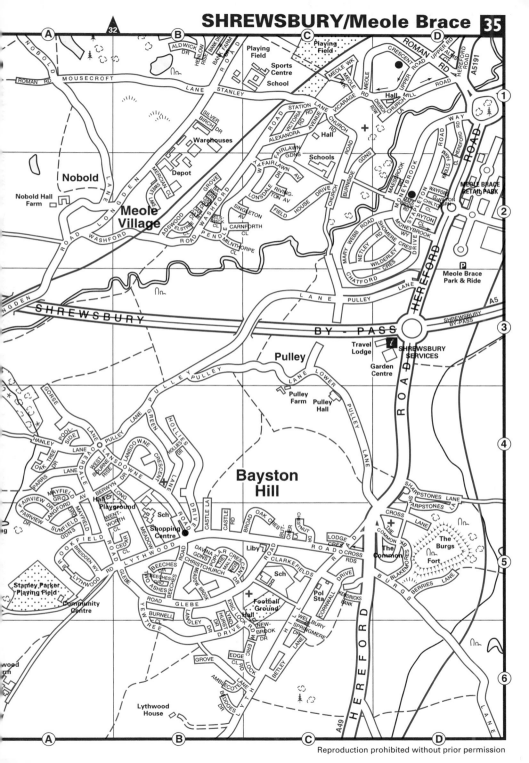

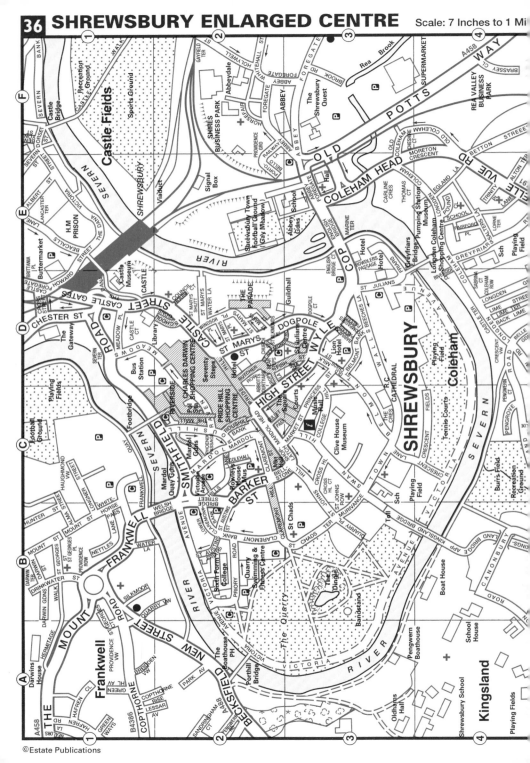

©Estate Publications

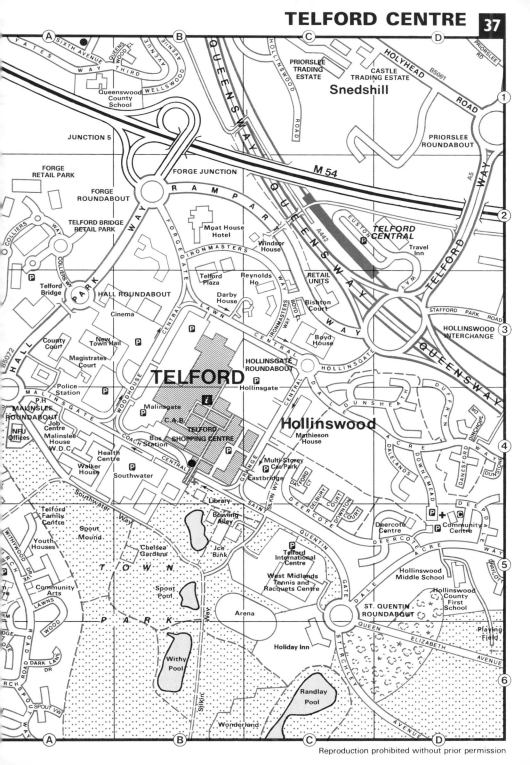

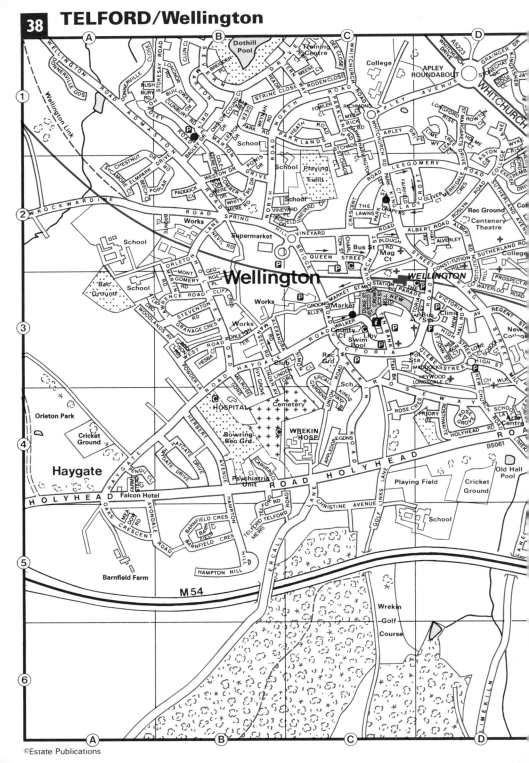

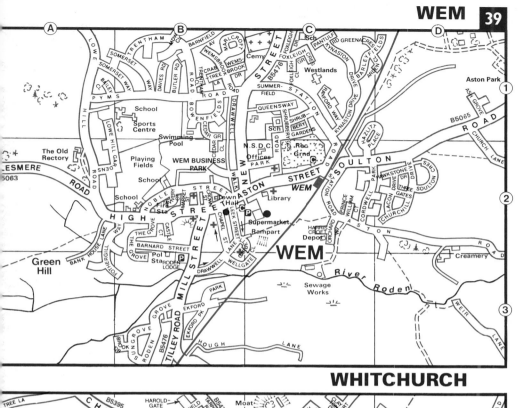

WHITCHURCH

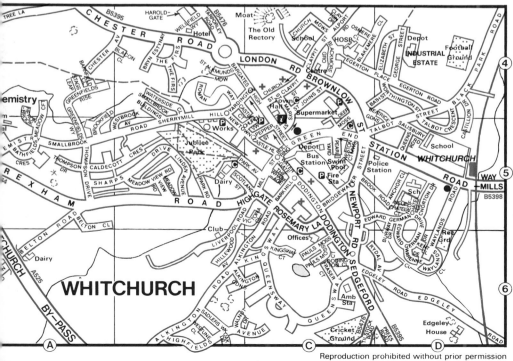

The Index includes some names for which there is insufficient space on the maps. These names are preceded by an * and are followed by the nearest adjoining thoroughfare.

ALBRIGHTON/ COSFORD

Abingdon Rd. WV7 13 E2
Abney Av. WV7 13 F5
Albert Rd. WV7 13 F6
Albrighton By-Pass. WV7 13 E3
Anson Rd. TF11 12 B4
Arrow Dri. WV7 13 G5
Ash Gro. WV7 13 F6
Ashfields. WV7 13 F6
Barclay Clo. WV7 13 G5
Barrington Clo. WV7 13 G5
Barton Lines. TF11 12 C3
Battle Rd. TF11 12 B4
Beechurst. WV7 13 F5
Bishton Rd. WV7 13 F6
Blenheim Cres. WV7 13 F2
Blue House La. WV7 13 G4
Botfield Clo. WV7 13 G5
Boulmer Av. TF11 12 D3
Bowlers Alley. TF11 12 C3
Bowling Grn La. WV7 13 E5
Breedon Clo. WV7 13 F5
Brindley Clo. WV7 13 G5
Brooklands Rd. WV7 13 G5
Buchan Av. TF11 12 D2
Bush Clo. WV7 13 G5
Bushfield Rd. WV7 13 F5
Cedar Dri. WV7 13 G5
Charles Av. WV7 13 F6
Cheshire Lines. TF11 12 C3
Chivenor Clo. WV7 13 F2
Church Rd. WV7 13 F6
Circular Rd. WV7 13 E2
Clock Mills. WV7 13 E5
Coningsby Rd. TF11 12 C3
Cordy La. WV7 13 H3
Cotswold Dri. WV7 13 G5
Cross Rd. WV7 13 F6
Delaware Av. WV7 13 E6
Donington Clo. WV7 13 G4
Eastern Av. WV7 13 E2
Elm Rd. WV7 13 E6
Fairlawn. WV7 13 G6
Fairlawn Ct. WV7 13 G6
Garridge Clo. WV7 13 F6
Grange Pk. WV7 13 F5
Grange Rd. WV7 13 F5
Green La. WV7 13 E6
Halifax Rd. WV7 13 G5
Harlech Way. WV7 13 G5
Harrow Cres. TF11 12 B3
Hereford Clo. WV7 13 E2
High St. WV7 13 F5
Honington Av. TF11 12 C2
Horsa Way. TF11 12 A4
Hudson Rd. TF11 12 B4
Kingswood Rd. WV7 13 H6
Kinloss Av. TF11 12 D2
Lancaster Clo. WV7 13 F2
Leeming Rd. TF11 12 C3
Leuchars La. TF11 12 C2
Loak Rd. WV7 13 E5
Locking Clo. WV7 13 E2
Long La. TF11 12 C2
Lyncroft. WV7 13 F6
Lysander Av. TF11 12 B4
Magister Rd. TF11 12 B4
Manor Gdns. WV7 13 G6
Marham Av. TF11 12 C2
Mayfair Clo. WV7 13 G5
Mayfield Rd. WV7 13 F6
Meadow Rd. WV7 13 G6
Meeson Clo. WV7 13 H6
Mill La. WV7 13 F2
Neachley La. TF11 12 A1
Newhouse La. WV7 13 F6
Newport Rd. WV7 13 E2
Newton Clo. WG11 13 E3

Old Hall Clo. WV7 13 F6
Old Worcester Rd. WV7 12 D5
Pitchford Rd. WV7 13 F6
Poplar Av. WV7 13 E2
Rectory Rd. WV7 13 F5
Redford Dri. WV7 13 F6
St Cuthberts Cres. WV7 13 E5
St Marys Clo. WV7 13 E5
Sandy La. WV7 13 E4
Saxon Park. WV7 13 F5
Shackerley La. WV7 13 F3
Shaw La. WV7 13 H5
Sheldon Ct. WV7 13 F6
Shifnal Rd. TF11 12 A5
Spitfire Av. TF11 12 B4
Station Rd. WV7 13 G6
Stirling Rd. WV7 13 F2
Swinderby Clo. WV7 13 E3
Sydnal La. WV7 13 E3
Talbot Rd. WV7 13 E6
Telford Av. WV7 13 G5
The Glebe. WV7 13 F6
The Limes. WV7 13 F6
The Orchard. WV7 13 F6
The Oval. WV7 13 E3
Valencia Rd. WV7 13 E3
Valiant Rd. WV7 13 E3
Victor Clo. WV7 13 E3
Victoria Rd. WV7 13 E3
Vincent Clo. WV7 13 E4
Virginia Rd. WV7 13 E3
Waddington Rd. TF11 12 C3
Wattisham Way. TF11 12 C3
Wellington Rd. WV7 13 F2
Western Av. WV7 13 E2
Weston Rd. WV7 13 G6
Whiston Clo. WV7 13 F5
White Ladies Ct. TF11 13 F5
Whitley Rd. TF11 12 B4
Windmill La. WV7 13 E6
Windsor Rd. WV7 13 G5
Wittering Rd. WV7 12 D3
Wolverley Ct. WV7 13 G6
Woodland Clo. WV7 13 G5
Worcester Rd. TF11 12 D3
Worthington Dri. WV7 13 E5
Wyton Av. TF11 12 C3

BISHOPS CASTLE

Billingsley Clo. SY9 16 B2
Bowling Grn Clo. SY9 16 B2
Brampton Rd. SY9 16 C3
Bull La. SY9 16 B1
Bull St. SY9 16 B1
Castle Green. SY9 16 B1
Castle St. SY9 16 B1
Chapel La. SY9 16 B2
Church Bank. SY9 16 B3
Church La. SY9 16 B3
Church St. SY9 16 B2
Clive House. SY9 16 B2
Copall Paddock. SY9 16 B2
Coricks Rise. SY9 16 A2
Corporation St. SY9 16 B3
Field La. SY9 16 B3
Fowl La. SY9 16 D1
Grange Gdns. SY9 16 A2
Grange Rd. SY9 16 B2
Harley Jenkins St. SY9 16 B2
High St. SY9 16 B2
INDUSTRIAL & RETAIL:
  Bishops Castle
    Business Park. SY9 16 C3
  Love La Ind Est. SY9 16 C2
Kerry Grn. SY9 16 A2
Kerry La. SY9 16 A2
Laburnum Alley. SY9 16 B1
Lacey Rd. SY9 16 A3
Lavender Bank. SY9 16 A2
Love La. SY9 16 C3
Market Sq. SY9 16 B2
New St. SY9 16 B2
Oak Meadow. SY9 16 B2
Pound Clo. SY9 16 B2
Salop St. SY9 16 B1
School La. SY9 16 B1

Schoolhouse La. SY9 16 C1
Station St. SY9 16 B2
The Novers. SY9 16 A3
The Ridge. SY9 16 A3
Union St. SY9 16 B2
Welsh St. SY9 16 A1
Woodbatch Rd. SY9 16 A3

BOMERE HEATH

Back La. SY4 16 B5
Baschurch Rd. SY4 16 A5
Bow Way. SY4 16 B4
Brook Rd. SY4 16 B4
Broomhall La. SY4 16 C5
Chapel Clo. SY4 16 B4
Cob Gro. SY4 16 B4
Cornfield Clo. SY4 16 B4
Croft Clo. SY4 16 B4
Dobell La. SY4 16 C5
Green Clo. SY4 16 C5
Green La. SY4 16 C5
Magnolia Clo. SY4 16 B6
Mere Clo. SY4 16 C5
Merrington Rd. SY4 16 B4
Preston Gubbals Rd. SY4 16 B5
Pump Rd. SY4 16 B4
Sefton Dri. SY4 16 B5
Shrewsbury Rd. SY4 16 B5
The Birches. SY4 16 B5
The Common. SY4 16 B5
The Crescent. SY4 16 B5
The Grove. SY4 16 B5
Wheathill Rise. SY4 16 C4
Whitehouse La. SY4 16 B5
Windsor La. SY4 16 C5
Yew Tree Bank. SY4 16 B5

BRIDGNORTH

Abbeyfield. WV16 14 A1
Abbotts Way. WV16 15 F2
Andersons La. WV16 14 C3
Ash Rd. WV16 14 B2
Avondale Clo. WV16 14 C4
Bank Steps. WV16 15 E4
Bank St. WV16 15 E4
Beaconsfield. WV16 14 B2
Beech Rd. WV16 14 B2
Beestons Clo. WV16 14 A3
Bernards Hill. WV15 15 F5
Birchlands. WV15 15 H4
Bowers Clo. WV16 14 A3
Bramble La. WV16 15 E2
Bramble Ridge. WV16 15 E2
Bridge St. WV15 15 E4
Bridgnorth By-Pass. WV16 14 A4
Brook Hollow. WV16 14 A4
Broseley Rd. WV16 14 D1
Campbell Clo. WV16 14 A4
Cann Hall Dri. WV15 15 F4
Cann Hall Rd. WV15 15 F4
Cantreyn Dri. WV16 14 C1
Captains Rd. WV16 14 C6
Cartway. WV16 15 E4
Castle Hill Walk. WV16 15 E5
Castle Ter. WV16 15 E4
Castlecroft. WV16 15 H5
Castlefields. WV16 14 B5
Church La. WV16 14 A3
Church St. WV16 15 E3
Claremont Dri. WV16 14 C2
Clee View Rd. WV16 14 A3
Cliff Rd. WV16 15 E3
College Ct. WV15 15 H6
Conduit La. WV16 14 B5
Copperfield. WV16 14 A1
Craig Walk. WV15 15 F5
Cricket Meadow. WV16 14 B2
Danesbridge. WV15 15 F6
Deighton Clo. WV16 14 C1
Dingle View. WV16 14 C1
Doctors La. WV15 15 F4
Duchess Dri. WV16 14 B1

Dunval Clo. WV16 14 B1
Dunval Rd. WV16 14 B1
East Castle St. WV16 15 E4
Elizabeth Av. WV16 14 B3
Elmhurst. WV15 15 H4
Fairfield. WV16 14 A2
Faraday Dri. WV15 15 H6
Farmlands Rd. WV16 14 A3
Firtrees. WV15 15 H5
Foster Rd. WV16 14 B1
Friars Lode. WV16 15 E3
Friars St. WV16 15 E3
Goldstone Dri. WV16 14 C1
Goodwood Av. WV15 15 G6
Granary Steps. WV16 15 E3
Greenfields Ct. WV16 14 C2
Greenfields Cres. WV16 14 C1
Greenfields Dri. WV16 14 C2
Greenfields Rd. WV16 14 C2
Greyfriars. WV16 15 E3
Grove Cres. WV15 15 G5
Harley Way. WV16 14 A4
Haughton Clo. WV16 14 A2
Hazel View. WV15 15 H5
Hermitage Clo. WV15 15 G4
High St. WV16 15 E3
Highfields Rd. WV16 14 A3
Highlands Rd. WV16 14 B5
Hillside Av. WV15 15 F6
Hilly Bank. WV16 14 D5
Hollybush Rd. WV16 14 C2
Hook Farm Rd. WV16 14 A2
Hospital St. WV15 15 F5
Huntsmans Clo. WV16 14 B4
INDUSTRIAL & RETAIL:
  Stanley Lane Ind Est. WV16 15 E1
Innage Cres. WV16 14 C2
Innage Gdns. WV16 14 D2
Innage La. WV16 14 C2
Kidderminster Rd. WV15 15 F6
King Charles Way. WV16 15 E2
Kings Loade. WV16 15 E5
Lavington View. WV15 15 F5
Leasowes Clo. WV16 14 A3
Linley View Rd. WV16 14 B1
Listley Ct. WV16 14 D4
Listley St. WV16 14 D4
Lodge La. WV16 15 G5
Love La. WV16 15 E1
Ludlow Heights. WV16 14 B5
Ludlow Rd. WV16 14 A6
Marchwood Clo. WV16 14 A1
Maudlins Clo. WV16 14 A4
Meadow Clo. WV16 14 C6
Meadway. WV15 15 F5
Mill St. WV15 15 F4
Moat St. WV16 15 E3
Morfe Rd. WV15 15 G4
Monks Ct. WV16 15 F4
New Rd. WV16 15 E5
Nicholas Cres. WV15 15 G5
North Gate. WV16 14 D3
Oak Gdns. WV16 14 B2
Oaklands. WV15 15 H5
Old Worcester Rd. WV15 15 H6
Oldbury Rd. WV16 15 E6
Oldbury Ter. WV16 14 D4
Oldbury Wells. WV16 14 C5
Orchard Clo. WV16 14 C2
Pale Meadow Rd. WV15 15 H5
Paulbrook Rd. WV16 14 C4
Pineway. WV15 15 H4
Pool Dri. WV16 14 A4
Portmans Way. WV16 14 A3
Postern Gate. WV16 15 E4
Pound St. WV16 14 D4
Princess Dri. WV16 14 B1
Priory Clo. WV15 15 F6
Priory Rd. WV15 15 G4
Queens Rd. WV15 15 G5
Queensway Dri. WV16 14 B1
Racecourse Dri. WV16 14 D2
Railway St. WV16 14 D4
Richmond Gdns. WV16 14 D2
Ridley Clo. WV16 14 A4
River Side. WV16 15 E4

Rose La. WV16 14 C4
Rosehill Dri. WV16 14 C4
Ryelands Gdns. WV16 14 B4
Sabrina Rd. WV15 15 F6
St James Dri. WV15 15 F4
St Johns St. WV15 15 F4
St Leonards Clo. WV16 15 E3
St Leonards Steps. WV16 15 E3
St Leonards Ter. WV16 15 E3
St Marys Clo. WV16 14 D4
St Marys Steps. WV16 15 E4
St Marys St. WV16 14 D4
St Nicholas Rd. WV15 15 G5
St Stephens Pl. WV16 15 F4
Salop St. WV16 14 C3
Severn Side Sth. WV15 15 F4
Severn St. WV15 15 F4
Springfield. WV15 15 F6
Squirrel Ct. WV16 14 D4
Stanley La. WV16 15 E1
Stoneway Steps. WV16 15 E4
Stourbridge Rd. WV15 15 F5
Stretton Clo. WV16 14 B5
Sydney Cottage Dri. WV16 14 B1
Tasley Clo. WV16 14 B3
Telford Rd. WV16 15 G2
The Cankhorn. WV16 15 E6
The Croft. WV15 15 F3
The Hawthorns. WV16 14 D5
The Hookfield. WV16 14 B2
The Mall. WV16 15 F5
The Wheatlands. WV16 14 A4
The Yards. WV16 14 D4
Three Ashes Rd. WV16 14 A3
Tining Clo. WV16 14 A4
Underhill St. WV16 15 E5
Uplands Dri. WV16 14 B5
Valley Ct. WV16 14 C4
Victoria Rd. WV16 14 B2
Wardle Clo. WV15 15 F5
Washbrook Rd. WV15 15 F5
Wellmeadow. WV15 15 F6
Wells Clo. WV16 14 C4
Wenlock Rd. WV16 14 A3
West Castle St. WV16 15 E5
Westgate. WV16 14 C3
Westgate Dri. WV16 14 B3
Westland Rd. WV16 14 B3
Wheatlands Rise. WV16 14 B4
Whitburn St. WV16 14 D4
Whitmore Clo. WV16 14 B1
Wolverhampton Rd. WV15 15 F4
Woodberry Clo. WV16 14 F3
Wrekin Rd. WV16 14 A3

CHURCH STRETTON

Alison Dri. SY6 17 D4
Alison Rd. SY6 17 D4
Ascot Clo. SY6 17 B3
Ashbrook Ct. SY6 17 B2
Ashbrook Cres. SY6 17 B2
Beaumont Ct. SY6 17 B3
Beaumont Rd. SY6 17 B4
Berwyn Clo. SY16 17 D5
Bodbury Clo. SY6 17 B2
Brooksbury. SY6 17 A3
Burway Rd. SY6 17 D5
Caradoc Dri. SY6 17 D5
Cardingmill Valley. SY6 17 A2
Central Av. SY6 17 B4
Chartwell Clo. SY6 17 B2
Chelmick Clo. SY6 17 C5
Chelmick Dri. SY6 17 C5
Church St. SY6 17 A4
Church Stretton By-Pass. SY6 17 B2
Church Way. SY6 17 A4
Churchill Rd. SY6 17 B2
Clive Av. SY6 17 B6
Coffin La. SY6 17 B4
Crossways. SY6 17 B4
Cunnery Rd. SY6 17 A4

Cunnery Ter. SY6 17 A4
Cwms La. SY6 17 D3
Easthope Rd. SY6 17 B4
Essex Rd. SY6 17 B4
Hazler Cres. SY6 17 C4
Hazler Dri. SY6 17 C4
Hazler Orchard. SY6 17 D5
Hazler Rd. SY6 17 C4
Helmeth Rd. SY6 17 C3
High St. SY6 17 A4
INDUSTRIAL & RETAIL:
Mynd Ind Est. SY6 17 B5
Kennedy Clo. SY6 17 B2
Kenyon Rd. SY6 17 B6
Kings Ct. SY6 17 B4
Lawney Clo. SY6 17 C3
Links Rd. SY6 17 A2
Lion Meadow. SY6 17 A4
Longhills Rd. SY6 17 A2
Longmynd Pl. SY6 17 B2
Ludlow Rd. SY6 17 A5
Lutwyche Clo. SY6 17 B3
Lutwyche Rd. SY6 17 B3
Madeira Walk. SY6 17 A2
Oakland Park. SY6 17 D4
Oaks Dri. SY6 17 D3
Oaks La. SY6 17 D3
Poplar Dri. SY6 17 C6
Rabbit Burrow. SY6 17 A1
Ragleth Rd. SY6 17 C5
Rectory Gdns. SY6 17 A3
St Lawrences Clo. SY6 17 A4
Sandford Av. SY6 17 B4
Sandford Rd. SY6 17 D4
Shrewsbury Rd. SY6 17 A3
Snatchfields La. SY6 17 C4
Stanyeld Rd. SY6 17 A2
Stretton Farm Rd. SY6 17 A5
Swains Mdw. SY6 17 A6
The Bridleways. SY6 17 C5
The Meadows. SY6 17 D5
The Paddock. SY6 17 B2
The Square. SY6 17 A4
The Yeld. SY6 17 B2
Trevor Hill. SY6 17 A2
Watling St Nth. SY6 17 C4
Watling St Sth. SY6 17 B6
Westfields. SY6 17 D5
Windle Hill. SY6 17 D5
Windsor Pl. SY6 17 C3
Woodcote Edge. SY6 17 A5
Yeld Bank. SY6 17 B1

CLEOBURY MORTIMER

Barkers La. DY14 18 C2
Barnfields. DY14 18 B3
Catherton Clo. DY14 18 A3
Catherton Rd. DY14 18 A2
Childe Rd. DY14 18 B3
Church St. DY14 18 C3
Collage Clo. DY14 18 B2
Curdale Clo. DY14 18 A3
Eagle La. DY14 18 B3
Fryers Clo. DY14 18 A3
Furlongs Clo. DY14 18 C1
Furlongs Rd. DY14 18 C1
Grove Meadow. DY14 18 D1
Hartman Clo. DY14 18 A3
Heath Clo. DY14 18 A3
High St. DY14 18 B3
INDUSTRIAL & RETAIL:
Cleobury Ind Est. DY14 18 B3
Lacon Clo. DY14 18 A3
Langland Rd. DY14 18 B1
Larks Rise. DY14 18 A3
Lea View. DY14 18 A2
Lion La. DY14 18 C3
Love La. DY14 18 B2
Lower Inhedge. DY14 18 D1
Lower St. DY14 18 B2
Ludlow Rd. DY14 18 A3
Mawley Clo. DY14 18 D1
Mill Pool Pl. DY14 18 D2
Mortimer Gdns. DY14 18 B2
Mortimer Hill. DY14 18 C3
New Rd. DY14 18 C2
New Rd Gdns. DY14 18 C2
Orchard End. DY14 18 C1
Pinkham. DY14 18 C2
*Ralph Jones Ter, Ludlow Rd. DY14 18 A3

Rockley Bank. DY14 18 C1
Ronhill Cres. DY14 18 C1
Ronhill La. DY14 18 C2
St Marys Pl. DY14 18 B2
Simon Evans Clo. DY14 18 C2
Station Rd. DY14 18 D1
Steeple Clo. DY14 18 B2
Talbot Sq. DY14 18 C3
Tenbury Mead. DY14 18 B3
Tenbury Rd. DY14 18 B3
The Hurst. DY14 18 C2
The Paddocks. DY14 18 B1
Vaughan Rd. DY14 18 B3
Viols Walk. DY14 18 C2
Woodland Rise. DY14 18 C1

CLUN

Bowls Grn. SY7 19 A2
Bridge St. SY7 19 B2
Buffalo La. SY7 19 A2
Castle St. SY7 19 A1
Church St. SY7 19 A3
Clun Bridge. SY7 19 A2
Craven Arms Rd. SY7 19 B2
Enfield St. SY7 19 A2
Farm Clo. SY7 19 B2
Ford St. SY7 19 B2
Hand Causeway. SY7 19 A3
Haslehurst Clo. SY7 19 B2
High St. SY7 19 B2
Hospital La. SY7 19 B1
INDUSTRIAL & RETAIL:
The Green Ind Est. SY7 19 D2
Kid La. SY7 19 B2
Knighton Rd. SY7 19 A3
Mount Pleasant. SY7 19 A3
Newport St. SY7 19 B2
Powells La. SY7 19 B2
Prospect Pl. SY7 19 B2
Riverside Dri. SY7 19 B2
Rock Hill. SY7 19 A3
St Georges Pl. SY7 19 A3
St Thomas's Clo. SY7 19 B2
School Rd. SY7 19 A3
The Square. SY7 19 B2
Turnpike Meadow. SY7 19 C2
Vicarage Rd. SY7 19 B3
Waterloo Dri. SY7 19 B2

CRAVEN ARMS

Albion Ter. SY7 18 B6
Ash Clo. SY7 18 B5
Brook Rd. SY7 18 B5
Brooklands Pk. SY7 18 B5
Burnside Clo. SY7 18 C6
Clun Rd. SY7 18 A6
Coppice Dri. SY7 18 B5
Coronation Rd. SY7 18 B5
Corvedale Rd. SY7 18 C6
Dale St. SY7 18 C6
Dodds La. SY7 18 C6
Fairfield Clo. SY7 18 C6
Greenfields Rd. SY7 18 B5
Halford Cres. SY7 18 C5
Halford Mdw. SY7 18 C5
Hawthorn Clo. SY7 18 B5
INDUSTRIAL & RETAIL:
Business Park. SY7 18 B4
Long La Ind Est. SY7 18 C6
Lambeth Clo. SY7 18 C6
Long La. SY7 18 A4
Ludlow Rd. SY7 18 B5
Maple Clo. SY7 18 B5
Market St. SY7 18 C6
Mayfield Av. SY7 18 C6
Meadow Rd. SY7 18 B5
Mynd Vw. SY7 18 C5
Newington Way. SY7 18 C4
Newton. SY7 18 C5
Newton St. SY7 18 C5
Norton View. SY7 18 C5
Oaks Rd. SY7 18 C5
Onnybrook Dri. SY7 18 C5
Park La. SY7 18 A6
St Johns Cres. SY7 18 B5
School Rd. SY7 18 B5
Shrewsbury Rd. SY7 18 C4
Station Cres. SY7 18 C5
Station Rd. SY7 18 C5

*Stoke Wood View, Dale St. SY7 18 C6
The Crescent. SY7 18 B5
Watling St. SY7 18 A6
White Meadow Clo. SY7 18 C5

ELLESMERE

Almond Dri. SY12 19 A5
Beech Dri. SY12 19 A6
Beech Gro. SY12 19 A5
Berwyn Vw. SY12 19 B6
Birch Rd. SY12 19 C5
Brownlow Cres. SY12 19 A4
Brownlow Pk. SY12 19 B5
Brownlow Rd. SY12 19 B5
Cambria Av. SY12 19 A5
Cedar Av. SY12 19 B5
Charlotte Row. SY12 19 B5
Cherry Dri. SY12 19 A5
Church Hill. SY12 19 C5
Church St. SY12 19 C5
Cross St. SY12 19 C5
Cygnet Ct. SY12 19 B4
David Philips Clo. SY12 19 A5
Diksmuide Dri. SY12 19 B4
Elm Clo. SY12 19 A5
Elson Rd. SY12 19 A4
Firtree Clo. SY12 19 A5
Grange Rd. SY12 19 A5
Greenways. SY12 19 A5
Grovesnor Cotts. SY12 19 B4
Heron Clo. SY12 19 B4
High St. SY12 19 B4
Hillcrest. SY12 19 C5
Holly Clo. SY12 19 A4
Kingfisher Wk. SY12 19 B4
Laburnum Dri. SY12 19 B4
Larch Dri. SY12 19 A5
Laurels Clo. SY12 19 B6
Levi Ct. SY12 19 A5
Lime Clo. SY12 19 A5
Love La. SY12 19 C6
Maple Av. SY12 19 A5
Market St. SY12 19 B5
Oak Dri. SY12 19 A5
Osprey Wk. SY12 19 C4
Oswestry Rd. SY12 19 A6
Pine Clo. SY12 19 A5
Pinfold St. SY12 19 B4
Railway Ter. SY12 19 B4
Robin Clo. SY12 19 B4
Rowan Clo. SY12 19 A5
St Johns Clo. SY12 19 C5
St Johns Hill. SY12 19 C5
Sandy La. SY12 19 C5
Scotland St. SY12 19 B5
Shrewsbury Rd. SY12 19 C5
Spar Bri. SY12 19 A6
Sparbridge La. SY12 19 A5
Spruce Clo. SY12 19 A5
Stanham Dri. SY12 19 B5
Station Rd. SY12 19 A4
Swan Hill. SY12 19 B5
Swanmere Ct. SY12 19 C4
Swanmere Pk. SY12 19 C4
Sycamore Cres. SY12 19 A5
Talbot La. SY12 19 C5
Talbot St. SY12 19 C5
Teal Dri. SY12 19 B4
The Hawthorns. SY12 19 A4
The Square. SY12 19 B5
Trimpley Ct. SY12 19 B5
Trimpley St. SY12 19 B5
Victoria St. SY12 19 B5
Watergate St. SY12 19 C5
Wharf Rd. SY12 19 B5
Willow Cres. SY12 19 B5
Willow St. SY12 19 B5

IRONBRIDGE/ BROSELEY

Anstice Rd. TF7 21 H1
Ashmore Cres. TF12 20 D4
Avenue Rd. TF7 21 E6
Balls La. TF8 21 E3
Barber St. TF7 20 D5
Barratts Hill. TF12 20 D5
Bath Rd. TF8 20 D2
Beech Dri. TF7 21 E6

Beech Rd. TF7 21 E1
Belle Vue Rd. TF8 20 D2
Belmont Rd. TF8 21 E2
Belvedere Gdns. TF8 21 F4
Benthall Hill. TF12 20 A5
Benthall View. TF7 21 F1
Birbeck Dri. TF7 21 F1
Birch Meadow. TF12 21 E5
Birch Row. TF12 21 E5
Blakeway Clo. TF12 21 F6
Bramblewood. TF12 21 E4
Brandywell Rd. TF12 21 E4
Bridge Bank. TF12 20 D3
Bridge Rd. TF12 20 D4
Bridgnorth Rd. TF12 21 E6
Buildwas Rd. TF8 20 B1
Calcutts Rd. TF8 21 F3
Canonbie Lea. TF7 21 G1
Cape St. TF12 20 D5
Carvers Rd. TF12 20 D5
Caughley Clo. TF12 21 F6
Chantry Clo. TF12 21 E4
Chapel La. TF12 20 D5
Chapel Rd, Ironbridge. TF8 21 E2
Chapel Rd, Jackfield. TF8 21 F3
Church St. TF12 21 E5
Coach Rd. TF8 20 C1
Coalford. TF8 21 F3
Coalport Clo. TF12 21 F6
Coalport High St. TF8 21 H3
Coalport Rd, Blists Hill, Madeley. TF7 21 H2
Coalport Rd, Broseley. TF12 21 F6
Coalport Rd, Coalport. TF8 21 H3
Cobwell Rd. TF12 20 D5
Cockshot La. TF12 21 F6
Collins Clo. TF12 21 F6
Coneybury Clo. TF12 21 F6
Coneybury Vw. TF12 21 F6
Cumberland Clo. TF12 20 D5
Dale End. TF8 20 C1
Dale Rd. TF8 20 C1
Dark La. TF12 21 E5
Delph Side. TF12 21 E5
Dove Ct. TF8 21 E2
Dovehouse Ct. TF12 21 E6
Duke St. TF12 20 D4
Earlswood Dri. TF7 21 G2
Easthope Rd. TF12 20 D3
Edinburgh Rd. TF12 20 D4
Elizabeth Cres. TF12 20 D4
Fairways Dri. TF7 21 G2
Ferry Rd. TF8 21 H4
Fielding Clo. TF12 21 F6
Floyer La. TF12 20 C4
Forbes Clo. TF7 21 E1
Forester Rd. TF12 21 E6
Foundry Ct. TF8 21 E6
Foundry La. TF12 21 E6
Fox La. TF12 20 D5
Glendinning Way. TF7 21 G1
Guest Rd. TF12 21 F6
Harris Grn. TF12 20 D5
Harris's La. TF8 21 E1
Harrison Clo. TF7 21 G1
Hermitage Way. TF7 21 G1
High St, Broseley. TF12 20 D5
High St, Ironbridge. TF8 20 D2
Hillside. TF8 21 E2
Hockley Rd. TF12 20 D6
Hodge Bower. TF8 20 D1
Hurst Clo. TF12 21 F6
Ironbridge Rd, Jackfield. TF8 21 E3
Ironbridge Rd, Madeley. TF7 21 F1
Jackfield Mill. TF8 21 H4
Jackson Av. TF12 20 D5
Jockey Bank. TF12 20 D4
King St. TF12 20 D4
Ladywood. TF8 20 D2
Langham Grn. TF7 21 G1
Lea Dingle. TF7 21 G2
Leasow. TF7 21 G2
Lees Farm Dri. TF7 21 G1
Legges Hill. TF12 20 D4
Legges Way. TF12 21 H2
Lincoln Hill. TF8 20 C2
Lloyds Head. TF8 21 F3

Lodge La, Benthall. TF12 20 C5
Lodge La, Ironbridge. TF8 20 D1
Lower Dingle. TF7 21 G2
Madeley Rd. TF8 21 E2
Madeley Wood View. TF7 21 G2
Maypole Rd. TF8 20 D3
Mellor Clo. TF7 21 G1
Mill La. TF12 20 D5
Miners Meadow. TF12 21 E6
New Bridge. TF8 21 F2
New Bridge Rd. TF8 21 E2
New Rd, Ironbridge. TF8 20 D2
New Rd, Madeley. TF7 21 H1
Orchard La. TF8 21 F1
Padmans Alley. TF12 20 D5
Paradise. TF8 20 C1
Park View. TF12 20 D6
Pound La. TF12 21 F6
Prestage Clo. TF12 21 F6
Quarry Rd. TF12 20 D4
Queen St. TF12 20 D5
Red La. TF8 21 H6
Redfield Rd. TF12 21 E4
Riddings Clo. TF12 21 F6
Roberts Rd. TF7 21 E1
Rough La. TF12 21 F6
Rowley Clo. TF7 21 G1
Saggars Clo. TF8 21 F2
St Lukes Rd. TF8 20 D2
St Marys Rd. TF8 21 F3
St Michaels Clo. TF7 21 H1
St Michaels Rd. TF7 21 H1
Salthouse Rd. TF8 21 G3
School Rd. TF7 21 E1
Severn Bank. TF8 20 D2
Severn Ter, Ironbridge. TF8 20 D2
Severn Ter, Jackfield. TF8 21 G3
Sherlock Hoy Clo. TF12 20 D6
Simpsons La. TF12 20 D4
Smithy Bank. TF12 20 D5
Somerset Clo. TF7 21 G1
South Dri. TF7 21 H1
Southorn Ct. TG12 20 D4
Speeds La. TF12 20 D5
Spout La. TF12 20 C3
Squires Clo. TF7 21 G2
Strethill Rd. TF8 20 C1
Swan St. TF12 20 D5
Sycamore Rd. TF12 20 D3
Tarbach Clo. TF12 21 F6
The Avenue. TF12 20 A4
The Bentlands. TF12 20 C4
The Knowle. TF8 21 F3
The Lloyds. TF8 21 F2
The Mines. TF12 20 D3
The Square. TF8 20 D2
The Wharfage. TF8 20 C1
Tontine Hill. TF8 20 D2
Underwood. TF12 21 E4
Upper Dingle Clo. TF8 21 G2
Upper Rd. TF7 21 H1
Waterloo St. TF8 21 E2
Wesley Rd. TF8 21 F2
Westerkirk Dri. TF7 21 G1
Whitehall Gdns. TF12 21 E6
Whitmore Clo. TF12 21 F6
Wilkinson Av. TF7 21 E6
Windsor Cres. TF12 20 D4
Woodhouse Rd. TF12 20 D5
Woodlands Dri. TF12 20 D3
Woodlands Grn. TF12 20 D4
Woodlands Rd. TF8 21 E2
Woodside Av. TF7 21 E1
Wrekin View. TF7 21 F1
Wyke La. TF12 20 A5
Yew Tree Rd. TF7 21 G2

LUDLOW

*Ashford Mews, Old St. SY8 22 D5
*Attorneys Walk, Bull Ring. SY8 22 D4
Baker Clo. SY8 23 G3
Ballard Clo. SY8 23 G3
Beech Clo. SY8 22 D1
Bell La. SY8 22 D5

Belle Vue Ter. SY8 22 D2
Blashfield Rd. SY8 23 G5
Bowdler Clo. SY8 23 G5
Brand La. SY8 22 D5
Bringewood Clo. SY8 22 D1
Bringewood Rise. SY8 22 D1
Bringewood Rd. SY8 22 D1
Broad St. SY8 22 C5
Bromfield Rd. SY8 22 B1
Bromley Rd. SY8 23 E3
Bull Ring. SY8 22 D4
Burway Clo. SY8 22 B1
Burway La. SY8 22 A1
Camp La. SY8 22 B5
Cangeford Dri. SY8 23 G3
Castle Sq. SY8 22 C5
Castle St. SY8 22 C5
Castle View Ter. SY8 22 D2
Castleford Rd. SY8 22 A1
Chandlers Clo. SY8 22 D5
Chapel Mews. SY8 22 D2
Chaple Row. SY8 22 D2
Charlton Rise. SY8 23 F5
Chestnut Gro. SY8 23 G5
Church St. SY8 22 C5
Church Walk. SY8 22 C4
Churchill Rd. SY8 23 F5
Clee View. SY8 23 F2
Clee View Clo. SY8 23 G3
Clifton Ct. SY8 22 D5
Coder Rd. SY8 23 H5
Coles Mdw. SY8 23 F6
Coles View. SY8 23 F6
College Ct. SY8 22 C4
College St. SY8 22 C4
Coronation Av. SY8 22 C2
Corve St. SY8 22 C3
Corve Vw. SY8 22 C2
Dark La. SY8 23 F4
Dinham. SY8 22 B5
Dinham Bri. SY8 22 B5
Dodmore La. SY8 22 D2
Downton View. SY8 23 F2
Elm Walk. SY8 22 D1
Fish St. SY8 22 C5
Fishmore Clo. SY8 22 C1
Fishmore Rd. SY8 22 C2
Fishmore Vw. SY8 22 C1
Foldgate La. SY8 23 H6
Foldgate Vw. SY8 23 G6
Friars Field. SY8 23 E5
Friars Gdn. SY8 22 D5
Friars Walk. SY8 22 D5
Glencoe Ter. SY8 22 D4
Gravel Hill. SY8 22 D4
Green Acres. SY8 23 G6
Guy Thornycroft Ct. SY8 23 G5
Halton La. SY8 22 A4
Hamlet Clo. SY8 23 E2
Hamlet Rd. SY8 23 E2
Harp La. SY8 22 C5
Hayton View. SY8 23 E2
Henley Orchards. SY8 23 E1
Henley Rd. SY8 23 E2
Henwick Ter. SY8 22 D2
High St. SY8 22 C5
Hillside. SY8 22 D3
Honey Meadow. SY8 23 G5
Hopton Clo. SY8 23 E1
Housman Av. SY8 23 F4
Housman Cres. SY8 23 F4
Hucklemarsh Rd. SY8 22 D1
INDUSTRIAL & RETAIL:
Burway Trading Est. SY8 22 B1
Ludlow Business Pk. SY8 23 H2
James Clo. SY8 23 E2
Jockey Flds. SY8 22 D5
Julian Rd. SY8 23 E3
Keepside Clo. SY8 22 A2
Kennet Bank. SY8 23 G5
Kershaw Clo. SY8 23 F1
Keyse Clo. SY8 23 G4
Keystone Gdns. SY8 23 E5
King St. SY8 22 C5
Lacy Rd. SY8 22 D2
Langford Clo. SY8 23 G5
Lime Clo. SY8 23 E1
Lingen Rd. SY8 23 G4
Linney. SY8 22 C3
Livesey Av. SY8 23 F3
Livesey Rd. SY8 23 E4
Lower Broad St. SY8 22 D6
Lower Fee. SY8 22 D6

Lower Galdeford. SY8 22 D4
Lower Mill St. SY8 22 C6
Lower Raven La. SY8 22 C5
Ludford Bridge. SY8 22 D6
Ludford Vw. SY8 23 G6
Ludlow By-Pass. SY8 23 E1
Maple Clo. SY8 23 E1
Market St. SY8 22 C5
Mary Elizabeth Rd. SY8 23 G6
Mayfields. SY8 22 C1
Middle Wood La. SY8 22 A5
Mill St. SY8 22 C5
Milton Rd. SY8 23 F4
*Mortimer Ct,
  Old St. SY8 22 D5
Mortimer Pl. SY8 23 F4
New Rd. SY8 22 C2
New St. SY8 22 D2
Normandie La. SY8 23 G4
Old St. SY8 22 D5
Orchard Gdns. SY8 23 E2
Orleton Rd. SY8 23 H5
Overton Rd. SY8 22 D6
Overton Vw. SY8 23 G6
Packer St. SY8 22 D4
Park Rd. SY8 22 D6
Parys Rd. SY8 23 G4
Pepper La. SY8 22 D5
Portcullis La. SY8 22 D4
Potter Clo. SY8 23 E1
Poyner Clo. SY8 23 E3
Poyner Rd. SY8 23 E3
Quality St. SY8 22 C4
Quarry Gdns. SY8 22 D3
Raven La. SY8 22 C5
Riddings Meadow. SY8 23 F4
Riddings Rd. SY8 23 F3
Rock La. SY8 23 E4
Rock Ter. SY8 23 F4
Rocks Grn. SY8 23 G1
Rocks Green Ter. SY8 23 G1
St John's La. SY8 22 D5
St John's Rd. SY8 22 D5
St Julians Av. SY8 23 E4
St Kellems. SY8 23 F5
St Margaret Rd. SY8 23 G3
St Marys La. SY8 22 C2
St Marys Mews. SY8 22 C2
St Peters Mws. SY8 22 D2
St Stephens Yd. SY8 22 D4
St Thomas's La. SY8 22 C5
Sandford Rd. SY8 23 F4
Sandpits Av. SY8 23 F4
Sandpits Clo. SY8 23 E2
Sandpits Rd. SY8 23 E2
Saunders Clo. SY8 22 D3
Shearman Rd. SY8 23 G4
Sheet Rd. SY8 23 E5
Shropshire Way. SY8 23 G4
Sidney Rd. SY8 23 F4
Silk Mill La. SY8 22 C5
Springfield Clo. SY8 22 D4
Stanton Clo. SY8 22 D1
Stanton Dri. SY8 22 D1
Stanton Rd. SY8 22 D1
Station Dri. SY8 22 D4
Steventon Cres. SY8 23 F6
Steventon Gdns. SY8 23 E5
Steventon New Rd. SY8 23 F5
*Streatley Mews,
  Corve St. SY8 22 C3
Summerfields. SY8 22 C1
Sycamore Clo. SY8 23 E1
Teme Av. SY8 22 D6
Teme Ter. SY8 22 D6
Temeside. SY8 22 D6
Temeside Gdns. SY8 23 E6
The Greyhound. SY8 23 E1
The Paddocks. SY8 23 F3
*The Vineyard, Lower
  Broad Street. SY8 22 D6
The Wildings. SY8 23 F3
Tollgate Rd. SY8 23 G5
Tower St. SY8 22 D4
Upper Fee. SY8 22 D6
Upper Galdeford. SY8 22 D4
Upper Linney. SY8 22 C4
Vashon Clo. SY8 23 G3
Weeping Cross La. SY8 23 E5
Westley Mews. SY8 22 C5
Weyman Rd. SY8 23 E1
Wheeler Rd. SY8 23 F3
Whitbatch Clo. SY8 22 C2
Whitbread Rd. SY8 23 F3
Whitcliffe Rd. SY8 22 A5
Whitefriars. SY8 23 E5

*Wood Yard,
  Bull Ring. SY8 22 D4

MARKET DRAYTON

Abbey Way. TF9 24 E3
Adderley Rd. TF9 24 C1
Alder Rd. TF9 24 A3
Alexandra Rd. TF9 24 B3
Allen Gdns. TF9 24 C3
Annefield Rd. TF9 24 E2
Ashbourne Dri. TF9 24 C2
Ashley Vw. TF9 24 C2
Ashwood Clo. TF9 24 A3
Aumbrey Clo. TF9 24 B3
Balmoral Rd. TF9 24 E2
Barrowstyles La. TF9 24 E2
Bartons La. TF9 24 B4
Bartons Rd. TF9 24 B4
Bentleys Rd. TF9 24 A4
Berrisford Clo. TF9 24 E3
Berrisford Rd. TF9 24 E3
Bert Smith Way. TF9 24 C1
Betton Rd. TF9 24 F2
Birch Clo. TF9 24 A4
Bridge Rd. TF9 24 B2
Bishops La. TF9 24 C2
Buntingsdale Rd. TF9 24 A4
Burgage Clo. TF9 24 D2
Buttercross. TF9 24 C3
Butts Rd. TF9 24 C3
Byron Clo. TF9 24 A4
Caernarvon Clo. TF9 24 E1
Campbell Rd. TF9 24 D2
Cedar Clo. TF9 24 B3
Cemetery Rd. TF9 24 C2
Chancel Dri. TF9 24 B3
Charles Way. TF9 24 B3
Charter Ct. TF9 24 D2
Cherry Way. TF9 24 E2
Cheshire St. TF9 24 D2
Chestnut Rd. TF9 24 B4
Christ Church La. TF9 24 B4
Church St. TF9 24 D3
Clifford Rd. TF9 24 C3
Clive Rd. TF9 24 C3
Coleridge Clo. TF9 24 B4
Combermere Ct. TF9 24 E2
*Corbet Ct,
  Manor Gdns. TF9 24 D3
Country Meadows. TF9 24 A3
Croft Way. TF9 24 B2
Cross St. TF9 24 D2
Cypress Clo. TF9 24 B3
Dalelands Est. TF9 24 C4
Dalelands West. TF9 24 B4
Dean Clo. TF9 24 B2
Dog Kennel La. TF9 24 D3
Drayton Gro. TF9 24 C2
Elizabeth Ct. TF9 24 C3
Ellesmere Gro. TF9 24 A3
Elm Dri. TF9 24 B3
Fairfields Rd. TF9 24 E1
Farcroft Dri. TF9 24 A3
Forest Rd. TF9 24 A3
*Frog La,
  Frogmore Rd. TF9 24 D2
Frogmore Rd. TF9 24 D2
Glendon Clo. TF9 24 A3
Goosefield Clo. TF9 24 C3
Great Hales St. TF9 24 E3
Greenfields La. TF9 24 C2
*Grosvenor Ct,
  Grosvenor Rd. TF9 24 E2
Grosvenor Rd. TF9 24 E2
Grotto Rd. TF9 24 B3
Grove Gdns. TF9 24 E3
Hampton Dri. TF9 24 E3
Hawthorn Way. TF9 24 E1
High St. TF9 24 D3
Hinsley Mill La. TF9 24 F2
Holly Clo. TF9 24 A3
Hospital La. TF9 24 B3
INDUSTRIAL & RETAIL:
Adderley Rd Ind Est. TF9 24 D1
Kenilworth Clo. TF9 24 E2
Kilnbank Cres. TF9 24 C4
Kilnbank Rd. TF9 24 D4
Kings Av. TF9 24 B3
Laburnum Clo. TF9 24 E1
Lime Gro. TF9 24 A4

*Linden Ct,
  Linden Way. TF9 24 E2
Linden Way. TF9 24 E2
Llewellyn Roberts Way. TF9 24 E1
Longford Gdns. TF9 24 A4
Longford Turning. TF9 24 A3
Longford Vw. TF9 24 A3
Longlands La. TF9 24 E2
Longslow Clo. TF9 24 B2
Longslow Rd. TF9 24 A1
Love La. TF9 24 D3
Maer La. TF9 24 D2
Manor Gdns. TF9 24 D3
Maple Clo. TF9 24 A4
Market Drayton By-Pass. TF9 24 A3
Marley Mount Cres. TF9 24 C2
Masefield Dri. TF9 24 B4
Meadow Clo. TF9 24 B2
Melrose Cres. TF9 24 B4
*Merchant Ct,
  Cheshire St. TF9 24 D2
Millfield Dri. TF9 24 F2
Millfield Grange. TF9 24 F2
Milton Dri. TF9 24 C1
Monksfield. TF9 24 D3
Mount La. TF9 24 D3
Newcastle Rd. TF9 24 F2
Newport Rd. TF9 24 D3
Newton Clo. TF9 24 C1
Newtown. TF9 24 D3
Norman Brook Ct. TF9 24 B3
Oakfield Rd. TF9 24 B3
*Oakview,
  Manor Gdns. TF9 24 D3
Orchard Rise. TF9 24 B3
Parker Bowles Dri. TF9 24 A3
Pezenas Dri. TF9 24 B2
Phoenix Bank. TF9 24 D3
Pine Clo. TF9 24 B3
Police Dri. TF9 24 C3
Portland Dri. TF9 24 B3
Priors La. TF9 24 B2
Priory Ct. TF9 24 B2
Prospect Rd. TF9 24 C2
Quarry Bank Rd. TF9 24 B4
Quarry House La. TF9 24 B4
Queen St. TF9 24 D2
Quorn Gro. TF9 24 A3
Red Bank. TF9 24 C3
Red Bank Cres. TF9 24 C3
Red Bank Rd. TF9 24 C3
Ridings Clo. TF9 24 C2
Rowan Rd. TF9 24 E2
Rush La. TF9 24 B2
St Marys St. TF9 24 D3
Salisbury Hill Vw. TF9 24 C3
Salisbury Rd. TF9 24 C3
Sambrook Cres. TF9 24 F2
Sandringham Clo. TF9 24 E1
Sandy La. TF9 24 D4
School La. TF9 24 A4
Sherwood Cres. TF9 24 A4
Shrewsbury Rd. TF9 24 A3
Shropshire St. TF9 24 D3
Simons Rd. TF9 24 B3
Smithfield Clo. TF9 24 D2
Smithfield Rd. TF9 24 D2
Stable La. TF9 24 B2
Stafford St. TF9 24 D2
Stuart Way. TF9 24 C1
Summerhill. TF9 24 C4
Summerhill Gdns. TF9 24 C4
Sutton Rd. TF9 24 C4
Sutton Way. TF9 24 C4
Sycamore Way. TF9 24 E1
Talbot Way. TF9 24 D1
Tennyson Dri. TF9 24 B4
Tern Ridge. TF9 24 E3
Tern Vw. TF9 24 B4
The Bridleway. TF9 24 B2
The Burgage. B TF9 24 D2
The Coppice. TF9 24 B2
The Lawns. TF9 24 E2
The Old Armoury. TF9 24 D3
The Oval. TF9 24 C3
The Paddocks. TF9 24 C2
The Quarry. TF9 24 B4
Tower Clo. TF9 24 C2
Towers Lawn. TF9 24 D2
Trout Ct. TF9 24 F2
Valley Vw. TF9 24 B4
Victoria Rd. TF9 24 C3
Walkmill Dri. TF9 24 D4

Walkmill Rd. TF9 24 D4
*Warren Ct,
  Shropshire St. TF9 24 D3
Warwick Dri. TF9 24 E1
Waterside Dri. TF9 24 F1
Westland Rd. TF9 24 B3
Westminster Dri. TF9 24 A4
Wilfred Own Clo. TF9 24 B4
*Wilkinson Walk,
  Cheshire St. TF9 24 D2
Willow Clo. TF9 24 A4
Windsor Dri. TF9 24 E1
Wordsworth Dri. TF9 24 A6

MUCH WENLOCK

Back La. TF13 25 D3
Barrow St. TF13 25 D2
Blakeway Hollow. TF13 25 A3
Bourton Rd. TF13 25 C4
Bridge Rd. TF13 25 C2
Bridgnorth Rd. TF13 25 D3
Bull Ring. TF13 25 D2
Carvers Croft. TF13 25 E3
Chapel Clo. TF13 25 D2
Dark La. TF13 25 C4
Forester Av. TF13 25 E3
George Shut. TF13 25 D3
Grenville Rd. TF13 25 F3
Havelock Cres. TF13 25 B3
High Causeway. TF13 25 C3
High St. TF13 25 D3
Hodgecroft. TF13 25 D3
Hunters Gate. TF13 25 E4
INDUSTRIAL & RETAIL:
Stretton Rd Ind Est. TF13 25 A4
King St. TF13 25 D3
Kingswood Clo. TF13 25 D1
Linden Av. TF13 25 D1
Manor House Clo. TF13 25 D3
Mutton Shut. TF13 25 D3
New Rd. TF13 25 D2
Oakfield Park. TF13 25 E3
Park Rd. TF13 25 E3
Portland Dri. TF13 25 F4
Priory Ct. TF13 25 D2
Queen St. TF13 25 D2
Racecourse Rd. TF13 25 D3
St Marys La. TF13 25 D3
St Marys Rd. TF13 25 D3
St Milburga Row. TF13 25 E3
St Owens Rd. TF13 25 D2
St Owens Well. TF13 25 D2
Sheinton St. TF13 25 D2
Shrewsbury Rd. TF13 25 A1
Smithfield Rd. TF13 25 D3
Southfield Rd. TF13 25 C3
Station Rd. TF13 25 D1
Station Wharf. TF13 25 D1
Stretton Rd. TF13 25 A4
Swan Meadow. TF13 25 E3
Sytche Clo. TF13 25 D1
The Crescent. TF13 25 D1
The Paddock. TF13 25 E3
The Square. TF13 25 D2
Victoria Rd. TF13 25 C3
Walton Av. TF13 25 D2
Wilmore St. TF13 25 D2

NEWPORT

Abbey Ct
  Shopping Arc. TF10 26 B2
Adams Cres. TF10 26 B2
Alton Gro. TF10 26 B9
Aqualate Clo. TF10 26 D2
Ashworth Way. TF10 26 C6
Aspen Way. TF10 26 C6
Aston Dri. TF10 26 B
Audley Av. TF10 26 C6
*Audley House Mws,
  Audley Av. TF10 26 D
Audley Rd. TF10 26 C
Avenue Rd. TF10 26 C
Avenue Rd Sth. TF10 26 C
Avondale. TF10 26 C
Barnmeadow Clo. TF10 26 D
Barnmeadow Rd. TF10 26 D
Beaumaris Rd. TF10 26 B
Beech Clo. TF10 26 C
Beechfields Way. TF10 26 C

Bellmans Yard. TF10	26 C3
Blackmere Clo. TF10	26 A4
Boughey Rd. TF10	26 B4
Bracken Way. TF10	26 C2
Broadway. TF10	26 D3
Brook Ho. TF10	26 B3
Brookside Av. TF10	26 B5
Broomfield Clo. TF10	26 A3
Broomfield Pl. TF10	26 A3
Broomfield Rd. TF10	26 A3
Burgage Ct. TF10	26 B3
Caldercrofts. TF10	26 C2
Chetwynd End. TF10	26 B3
Chetwynd Gro. TF10	26 B2
Chetwynd Rd. TF10	26 B1
Church Sq. TF10	26 B3
Coppice Dri. TF10	26 B1
Cornmell Lea. TF10	26 C3
Daniels Cross. TF10	26 D3
Deer Park Dri. TF10	26 B1
Drovers Way. TF10	26 D2
Dungarven Dri. TF10	26 A4
Edgmond Rd. TF10	26 A2
Elkington Clo. TF10	26 B4
Ellismere Ct. TF10	26 B4
Elm Clo. TF10	26 C5
Fair Oak. TF10	26 C2
Fallow Deer Lawn. TF10	26 B1
Farm Gro. TF10	26 A3
Farriers Grn. TF10	26 D3
Fishers Lock. TF10	26 C2
Ford Rd. TF10	26 A4
Forton Glade. TF10	26 C1
Forton Rd. TF10	26 B2
Gilbert Clo. TF10	26 B4
Granville Av. TF10	26 C4
Granville Clo. TF10	26 C4
Granville Rd. TF10	26 B4
Gravelly Dri. TF10	26 B4
Green La. TF10	26 B2
Greenacres Way. TF10	26 A3
Greenfield Ter. TF10	26 D5
Greenvale. TF10	26 B6
Hallcroft Clo. TF10	26 B3
Hallcroft Gdns. TF10	26 B3
Hampton Clo. TF10	26 D3
Hampton Dri. TF10	26 C2
Harcourt Dri. TF10	26 D2
Havisham Ct. TF10	26 B3
Hawkstone Av. TF10	26 B4
Heathwood Rd. TF10	26 B4
Henley Dri. TF10	26 D2
Heron Way. TF10	26 C1
High Meadows. TF10	26 D3
High St. TF10	26 B3
Highfield. TF10	26 C6
Highland Rd. TF10	26 B4
INDUSTRIAL & RETAIL:	
Audley Av Ind Est. TF10	26 D4
Springfields Ind Est. TF10	26 C5
Ingestre Clo. TF10	26 A4
Islington Clo. TF10	26 C2
Jethros Croft. TF10	26 D1
Juniper Row. TF10	26 C5
Kestrel Clo. TF10	26 C1
Kingfisher Clo. TF10	26 C1
Lapworth Way. TF10	26 C3
Laurel Dri. TF10	26 C3
Leigh Rd. TF10	26 B4
Little Hales Rd. TF10	26 D6
Longford Rd. TF10	26 A4
Lower Bar. TF10	26 B3
Masons Pl. TF10	26 B2
Maynards Croft. TF10	26 C2
Meadow Rd. TF10	26 C3
Meadow View Clo. TF10	26 D3
Meadow View Rd. TF10	26 D3
Mere Clo. TF10	26 C2
Moorfield La. TF10	26 A4
Moorland Rd. TF10	26 A4
Mulberry Clo. TF10	26 C5
New St. TF10	26 B3
Newport By-Pass. TF10	26 D1
Newport Rd. TF10	26 A2
Newtown. TF10	26 B5
Norbroom Ct. TF10	26 D2
Norbroom Dri. TF10	26 D2
Oak Av. TF10	26 B5
Orchard Clo. TF10	26 B6
Park End. TF10	26 B1
Pave La. TF10	26 D6
Pen-y-Bryn Way. TF10	26 C4
Pinewoods. TF10	26 B6
Plough La. TF10	26 C1
Ploughmans Croft. TF10	26 D2
Powell Pl. TF10	26 C3
Primrose Dri. TF10	26 C5
Princess Gdns. TF10	26 C5
Queens Dri. TF10	26 C5
Richmond Clo. TF10	26 C5
Roddham Ct. TF10	26 B4
Roe Deer Grn. TF10	26 B1
Rowan Dri. TF10	26 C5
St Andrews Way. TF10	26 B6
St Mary St. TF10	26 B3
Salters Ct. TF10	26 B3
Salters La. TF10	26 B3
Sandiford Cres. TF10	26 B4
Sandycroft. TF10	26 C3
School Grove La. TF10	26 D3
Shepherds Ct. TF10	26 D2
Shrewsbury Way. TF10	26 B4
Shuker Clo. TF10	26 C4
Silverdale Clo. TF10	26 B5
Springfield Av. TF10	26 B5
Springfields. TF10	26 C4
Stafford Rd. TF10	26 C3
Stafford St. TF10	26 C3
Station Ct. TF10	26 C5
Station Rd. TF10	26 C4
Station Ter. TF10	26 C5
Stretton Av. TF10	26 B4
Strine Way. TF10	26 C2
Summerhouse Gro. TF10	26 C2
Swanmere. TF10	26 C1
Talbot Clo. TF10	26 A4
Tan Bank. TF10	26 C3
The Close. TF10	26 B6
The Crescent. TF10	26 C6
The Dale. TF10	26 C6
The Larches. TF10	26 B4
The Oval Bungalows. TF10	26 C3
The Spinney. TF10	26 C6
Town Wells. TF10	26 C5
*Tuckers Pl, High St. TF10	26 B3
Tudor Clo. TF10	26 C2
Underhill Clo. TF10	26 C3
Upper Bar. TF10	26 C4
Vauxhall Cres. TF10	26 B4
Vauxhall Ter. TF10	26 B3
Victoria Pk. TF10	26 C3
Vineyard Dri. TF10	26 C3
Vineyard Rd. TF10	26 C3
Wallshead Way. TF10	26 B6
Walnut Clo. TF10	26 C5
Water La. TF10	26 B3
Waterford Dri. TF10	26 A5
Waterside Mews. TF10	26 B3
Wellington Rd. TF10	26 A6
Wenlock Dri. TF10	26 B4
Wrekin Av. TF10	26 B4

OSWESTRY

*Albert Pl, Beatrice St. SY11	27 C2
Albert Rd. SY11	27 C1
Albion Hill. SY11	27 C2
Alexandra Rd. SY11	27 B1
Ambleside Rd. SY11	27 C2
Ardmillan Clo. SY11	27 D2
Ardmillan Ct. SY11	27 D2
Ardmillan La. SY11	27 D2
Arthur St. SY11	27 B2
Arundel Rd. SY11	27 B2
Ascot Rd. SY11	27 E1
Ash Rd. SY11	27 C1
Aston Clo. SY11	27 F2
Aston Way. SY11	27 F2
Bailey Head. SY11	27 C2
Bailey St. SY11	27 C2
Balmoral Clo. SY11	27 E2
Balmoral Cres. SY11	27 E2
Barnfield Clo. SY11	27 C3
Beatrice St. SY11	27 C2
Beech Gro. SY11	27 D2
Black Gate St. SY11	27 C2
Blackfriars. SY11	27 E2
Blenheim Clo. SY11	27 E1
Border Clo. SY11	27 D3
Bradley Fields. SY11	27 A2
Breidden Clo. SY11	27 A3
Bridgeman Rd. SY11	27 C2
Broad Walk. SY11	27 B2
Broadlands Way. SY11	27 F2
Brookhouse Rd. SY11	27 C2
Broom Hall Clo. SY11	27 A3
Broomhall La. SY11	27 A3
Bryn Rise. SY11	27 A2
Brynhafod Dri. SY11	27 A2
Brynhafod La. SY11	27 A2
Brynhafod Rd. SY11	27 B2
Buckingham Clo. SY11	27 E2
Cabin La. SY11	27 E2
Caer Rd. SY11	27 C1
Cambrian Dri. SY11	27 D1
Cambrian Pl. SY11	27 C2
Campbell Cl. SY11	27 F2
Castle Fields. SY11	27 C2
Castle St. SY11	27 B2
Chapel St. SY11	27 B2
Chaucer Clo. SY11	27 E2
Chaucer Rd. SY11	27 E2
Cherry Tree Dri. SY11	27 D3
Chestnut Av. SY11	27 D3
*Clandd Du, Willow St. SY11	27 C2
Church Ct. SY11	27 B3
Church St. SY11	27 B3
Church Vw. SY11	27 B2
College Rd. SY11	27 E3
*Combs La Ville Clo, Guinevere Clo. SY11	27 D1
Coney Grn. SY11	27 C2
Coppice Dri. SY11	27 D1
Crampton Ct. SY11	27 F2
Cranbrook Dri. SY11	27 B1
Crestwood Ct. SY11	27 C2
Croeswylan Clo. SY11	27 A4
Croeswylan Cres. SY11	27 B4
Croeswylan La. SY11	27 A4
Cross St. SY11	27 C2
Croxon Rise. SY11	27 F2
Denham Dri. SY11	27 B1
Diamond Av. SY11	27 F2
Eaton Fields. SY11	27 F2
Edward St. SY11	27 B3
Elgar Clo. SY11	27 D2
Elm Clo. SY11	27 E3
English Walls. SY11	27 C2
Epsom Clo. SY11	27 E1
Ferrers Rd. SY11	27 C3
Festival Sq. SY11	27 C2
Ffynnon Ct. SY11	27 C3
Ffynnon Gdns. SY11	27 C3
Findon Dri. SY11	27 B1
Fir Gro. SY11	27 D3
Fitzalan Rd. SY11	27 A2
Fort Vw. SY11	27 C1
Friars Av. SY11	27 E2
Friars Clo. SY11	27 E2
Gatcombe Gdns. SY11	27 F2
Gate St. SY11	27 C1
Gateacre Av. SY11	27 C1
Gateacre Rd. SY11	27 C1
Gittin St. SY11	27 C1
Glentworth Av. SY11	27 B4
Glentworth Clo. SY11	27 B4
Glentworth Dri. SY11	27 B4
*Glentworth Gdns, Glentworth Clo. SY11	27 B4
Glentworth Rise. SY11	27 B4
Glovers Meadow. SY11	27 D4
Gobowen Rd. SY11	27 C1
Gower Pl. SY11	27 D2
Green End. SY11	27 B1
Greenbank Clo. SY11	27 C2
Greyfriars. SY11	27 E2
Greystones Way. SY11	27 D4
Grosvenor Rd. SY11	27 F1
Guinevere Clo. SY11	27 D1
Hafod Clo. SY11	27 A2
Hampton Clo. SY11	27 A2
Hampton Fields. SY11	27 A2
Hampton Rise. SY11	27 A2
Hampton Rd. SY11	27 A2
Harlech Rd. SY11	27 E1
Hawthorn Gro. SY11	27 D3
Hazel Gro. SY11	27 D3
Heather Clo. SY11	27 E3
Henley Dri. SY11	27 F1
Henry Jones Rd. SY11	27 F2
High Fawr Av. SY11	27 A2
High Fawr Clo. SY11	27 A2
High Grove. SY11	27 F2
High Lea Clo. SY11	27 A2
Hillside. SY11	27 C1
Holbache Rd. SY11	27 B2
Holly Grn. SY11	27 D3
Horsemarket. SY11	27 C2
Hurdsman St. SY11	27 B1
INDUSTRIAL & RETAIL:	
Glovers Meadow Ind Est. SY11	27 E4
Mile End Business Pk. SY11	27 E4
Jasmine Clo. SY11	27 D1
Jasmine Gdns. SY11	27 D1
Jemmett Pl. SY11	27 B3
Jennings Rd. SY11	27 A2
Kay Clo. SY11	27 F2
Kensington Clo. SY11	27 E1
King St. SY11	27 C2
Knightsway. SY11	27 D1
Laburnum Dri. SY11	27 D3
Langland Rd. SY11	27 D2
Leg St. SY11	27 C2
Lilac Gro. SY11	27 E3
Lime Gro. SY11	27 D3
Liverpool Rd. SY11	27 C1
Liverpool Rd West. SY11	27 B1
Llanforda Clo. SY11	27 A2
Llanforda Mead. SY11	27 A2
Llanforda Rise. SY11	27 A3
Lloyd St. SY11	27 C1
Llwyn Fields. SY11	27 C1
Llwyn Rd. SY11	27 C1
Llys Av. SY11	27 E2
Llys Clo. SY11	27 E3
Llys Ct. SY11	27 E2
Llys La. SY11	27 C2
Llys Pl. SY11	27 E3
Llys Rd. SY11	27 E2
Longueville Dri. SY11	27 F2
Lord St. SY11	27 C2
Lorne St. SY11	27 C1
Love La. SY11	27 B4
Lower Brook St. SY11	27 B3
Lower Hafod. SY11	27 A2
Lower Minster. SY11	27 A2
*Madog Pl, Beatrice St. SY11	27 C2
Maes-y-Clywdd. SY11	27 F4
Maesbury Rd. SY11	27 D4
Malory Rd. SY11	27 D2
Maple Av. SY11	27 E3
Maplehurst Dri. SY11	27 E1
Maserfield. SY11	27 A3
Maserfield Clo. SY11	27 A3
Meadow Clo. SY11	27 E1
Meadow Lea. SY11	27 E1
Meadow Rise. SY11	27 E1
Middleton Clo. SY11	27 E2
Middleton Rd. SY11	27 E2
Minshall Pl. SY11	27 F2
Monkmoor Av. SY11	27 D2
Monkmoor Clo. SY11	27 D2
Monkmoor Ct. SY11	27 D1
Monkmoor Rd. SY11	27 D2
Morda Clo. SY11	27 B2
Morda Rd. SY11	27 B4
Mount Clo. SY11	27 B1
Mount Cres. SY11	27 A1
Mount Dri. SY11	27 B2
Mount Rd. SY11	27 A1
New Park Rd. SY11	27 E1
New St. SY11	27 B2
*Newgate Ct, Church St. SY11	27 B3
Oak Dri. SY11	27 D3
Oak St. SY11	27 B2
Oakhurst Av. SY11	27 B1
Oakhurst Rd. SY11	27 B1
Oerley Clo. SY11	27 A2
Oerley Way. SY11	27 A2
Offa Dri. SY11	27 D1
Old Fort Rd. SY11	27 C1
Orchard St. SY11	27 C2
Osbourne Clo. SY11	27 F2
Oswald Rd. SY11	27 C2
*Oswald Mews, Oswald Well La. SY11	27 B3
Oswalds Pl. SY11	27 B3
Oswalds Well La. SY11	27 A3
Oswestry By-Pass. SY11	27 F1
Park Av. SY11	27 B2
Park Dri. SY11	27 B1
Park St. SY11	27 C3
Park Ter. SY11	27 D1
Park St Clo. SY11	27 C3
Penylan La. SY11	27 A4
Pine Gro. SY11	27 D3
Plas Fynnan Way. SY11	27 D2
Pool Rd. SY11	27 B4
*Porkington Ter, Willow St. SY11	27 B2
Powis Av. SY11	27 D2
Powis Pl. SY11	27 C2
Prince Charles Clo. SY11	27 E2
Prince Charles Rd. SY11	27 E2
Prince St. SY11	27 C2
Queen Elizabeth Clo. SY11	27 D1
Queen Elizabeth Dri. SY11	27 D1
Queens Clo. SY11	27 C3
Queens Pk. SY11	27 C3
Queens Rd. SY11	27 C3
Radfords Field. SY11	27 D4
Regent Ct. SY11	27 C3
Roft St. SY11	27 C3
Roundwood Clo. SY11	27 F2
St James Clo. SY11	27 E2
St Johns Ct. SY11	27 C3
Salop Rd. SY11	27 C3
Sandringham Av. SY11	27 E1
School Vw. SY11	27 B3
Sefton Pl. SY11	27 B1
Shelf Bank Clo. SY11	27 D1
Shrewsbury Rd. SY11	27 D3
Sleepy Hollow. SY11	27 A2
Smale Rise. SY11	27 F2
Smithfield Rd. SY11	27 C3
Smithfield St. SY11	27 B2
South View. SY11	27 B1
Southgate Clo. SY11	27 D3
Stewart Rd. SY11	27 C3
Summerfield Clo. SY11	27 E2
Swan La. SY11	27 C1
Sycamore Dri. SY11	27 D3
The Cross. SY11	27 C2
The Green. SY11	27 D3
Thornhurst Av. SY11	27 B1
Trefonen Rd. SY11	27 A4
Trinity Ct. SY11	27 C3
Ty-Maen. SY11	27 B3
Unicorn Rd. SY11	27 D1
Upper Ash Rd. SY11	27 B1
Upper Brook St. SY11	27 A3
Upper Church St. SY11	27 B3
Upper Lord St. SY11	27 B1
Victoria Clo. SY11	27 C3
Victoria Cres. SY11	27 C3
Victoria Fields. SY11	27 C3
Victoria Grn. SY11	27 C3
Victoria Rd. SY11	27 C3
Victoria St. SY11	27 C3
Viscount Bridgeman Ct. SY11	27 D1
Vyrnwy Pl. SY11	27 B1
Vyrnwy Rd. SY11	27 B1
Walford Rd. SY11	27 D2
Watkin Dri. SY11	27 A3
Wats Dri. SY11	27 D1
Wedge Mews. SY11	27 E3
Welsh Walls. SY11	27 B2
West St. SY11	27 B3
Western Dri. SY11	27 D1
Weston Av. SY11	27 B3
Weston La. SY11	27 B4
Whitefriars. SY11	27 E2
Whiteminster. SY11	27 A3
Whitfield Clo. SY11	27 F2
Whittington Rd. SY11	27 D1
Wilfred Owen Av. SY11	27 E2
Wilfred Owen Clo. SY11	27 E3
Wilfred Owen Rd. SY11	27 E3
Willow St. SY11	27 B2
Wilmot Dri. SY11	27 B4
Wilmot Rd. SY11	27 B4
Windsor Clo. SY11	27 E1
Windsor Rd. SY11	27 E1
Woodlands Clo. SY11	27 D3
Woodside. SY11	27 C1
York Fields. SY11	27 B1
York St. SY11	27 B1

45

Oriel Way. SY3 34 C5
Oswell Rd. SY3 31 E6
Oteley Rd. SY2 32 C6
Outwood. SY1 30 D1
Overcross. SY3 32 D5
Overdale Rd. SY3 35 A4
Overstone. SY1 30 D1
Overton Clo. SY1 31 H3
Painters Pl. SY3 34 B1
Park Av. SY3 36 A2
Parrs La. SY3 35 A4
Partridge Clo. SY1 31 H2
Patricia Dri. SY2 33 G3
Peace Dri. SY2 33 F2
Peacehaven. SY1 31 h2
Pemberton Way. SY3 32 D4
Pembroke Way. SY3 34 D4
Pendle Way. SY3 35 B2
Pengrove. SY3 36 C4
Pengwern Ct. SY3 36 C4
Pengwern Clo. SY3 32 A2
Pengwern Rd. SY3 32 A2
Percy St. SY3 30 C6
Percy St North. SY1 30 C6
Perivale Clo. SY3 34 D4
Phoenix Pass. SY1 36 C2
Pig Trough. SY1 30 C6
Pinewood Clo. SY1 30 C3
Pitchford Rd. SY1 30 D2
Pool Rise. SY2 33 E5
Poolside. SY2 35 A4
Poplar Cres. SY3 35 B5
Porchfield. SY2 33 F1
Porthill Clo. SY3 34 D2
Porthill Dri. SY3 34 D2
Porthill Gdns. SY2 32 A2
Porthill Rd. SY3 32 A2
Portland Cres. SY2 33 F2
Portobello. SY2 36 E2
Potters Meadow. SY2 33 F1
Pound Clo. SY3 36 E4
Pountney Gdns. SY3 32 C3
Powis Dri. SY1 30 D4
Poynton Dri. SY1 30 D3
Prescott Clo. SY2 33 F6
Prestbury Grn. SY1 31 E2
Preston St. SY3 33 F3
Pride Hill. SY1 36 C2
Pride Hill Shopping
  Centre. SY1 36 C2
Primrose Dri. SY3 32 D5
Princess St. SY1 36 C3
Priory Dri. SY3 32 A5
Priory Ridge. SY3 32 A5
Priory Rd. SY1 36 B2
Pritchard Way. SY3 33 E4
Providence Vw. SY3 36 A1
Pulley La. SY3 35 B4
Pulrose Walk. SY3 32 D5
Quarry Pl. SY3 36 B3
Quatford Clo. SY1 31 H3
Queen St. SY1 32 D1
Quinton Clo. SY3 34 B1
Raby Cres. SY3 32 C4
Racecourse Av. SY2 33 E2
Racecourse Cres. SY3 33 E1
Racecourse Grn. SY2 33 E1
Racecourse La. SY3 34 A1
Rad Valley Gdns. SY3 34 C3
Rad Valley Rd. SY3 34 C3
Radbrook Rd. SY3 34 C4
Ragleth Gdns. SY2 33 F2
Railway La. SY2 36 F2
Ramsey Mdws. SY1 31 G2
Raven Meadows 36 C2
*Ravenscourt Walk
  Falcons Way. SY3 34 B3
Ravenscroft Gdns. SY2 33 E1
Rea St. SY3 32 D4
Reabrook Av. SY3 33 E4
Red Barn La. SY3 32 B4
Redfern Clo. SY3 32 D5
Redfield. SY1 30 C4
Reedham Rd. SY1 31 E6
Regents Dri. SY1. SY1 31 E6
Reynaulds Clo. SY3 33 G3
Richard Onslow Ct.
  SY2 31 F6
Richmond Dri. SY3 34 D2
Riders Lea. SY3 34 D3
Ridgebourne Rd. SY3 34 D3
Ripple Clo. SY3 33 F6
Riverdale Rd. SY3 31 F6
Riverside. SY1 36 C2
Rivington Av. SY3 35 C2
Robertson Way. SY1 31 E6

Robin Clo. SY1 31 H2
Rocke St. SY3 32 D4
Rocke Walk. SY2 32 D3
Roman Rd,
  Nobold. SY3 35 A1
Roman Rd,
  Shrewsbury. SY3 32 A4
Romsley Dri. SY2 33 E5
Rosedale. SY1 31 F3
Roselyn. SY1 31 F3
Rosemede. SY1 31 F3
Roseway. SY1 31 F3
Rotherfield. SY1 31 E4
Rothley Clo. SY3 34 D4
Roundhill Clo. SY1 30 B6
Roundhill Grn. SY1 30 B6
Roundhill La. SY1 30 B5
Roundway. SY3 32 D5
Roushill. SY1 36 C2
Roushill Bank. SY1 36 C2
Rowley Ct. SY2 33 E6
Rowton Rd. SY2 33 E6
Rushbrooke Way. SY2 31 G5
Rushton Rd. SY3 31 F6
Russell Field. SY3 34 D3
Russell Ridge. SY3 34 D3
Rutland. SY1 31 E1
Rydal Av. SY1 31 E3
Ryelands. SY3 34 C4
Ryton Clo. SY3 35 D2
Sabrina Ct. SY3 32 D4
St Alkmunds Pl. SY1 36 D2
St Alkmund Sq. SY1 36 D2
St Andrews Rd. SY3 34 C4
St Annes Rd. SY3 34 C5
St Antonys Rd. SY3 34 C4
St Austin Friars. SY1 36 B2
St Austins St. SY1 36 B2
St Catherines Dri. SY3 34 C4
St Chads Ter. SY1 36 A1
St Georges Ct. SY3 36 A1
St Georges Pl. SY3 36 B1
St Georges St. SY3 36 B1
St Giles Rd. SY2 33 E2
St James Rd. SY2 33 G2
St Johns Hill. SY1 36 B3
St Johns Row. SY1 36 B3
St Julians Friars. SY1 36 D3
St Marys Ct. SY1 36 D2
St Marys Pl. SY1 36 D2
St Marys Shutt. SY1 36 D2
St Marys St. SY1 36 D2
St Marys Water La. SY1 36 D2
St Michaels Gate. SY1 30 D6
St Michaels St. SY1 30 D6
St Michaels Ter. SY1 30 D6
Salamanca Av. SY3 34 C3
Salcombe Dri. SY2 33 G6
Salendine. SY1 30 C4
Saltdean Dri. SY2 33 G6
Salters La. SY3 36 E4
Saltney Clo. SY2 33 G5
Sambrook Clo. SY1 30 D4
Sandford Av. SY1 30 D4
Sandford Clo. SY1 30 D4
Sandiway. SY1 34 C3
Sandleigh. SY3 34 B1
Sandown Cres. SY3 34 A1
Sandringham Ct. SY3 32 A2
Sandygate Av. SY2 33 E5
Sawston Clo. SY3 34 C4
Saxon Ct. SY3 34 A2
School Gdns. SY3 36 D2
School La. SY3 36 E4
Scott St. SY3 32 D4
Seabury Clo. SY3 32 D4
Sedgeford Dri. SY2 33 G3
Selwyn Clo. SY3 32 D5
Severn Bank. SY1 32 D1
Severn St. SY1 32 D1
Severn Ter. SY1 36 D1
Shackleton Way. SY3 34 A2
Sharpstones La. SY3 35 A3
Shaw Rd. SY3 33 F1
Shelton Fields. SY1 34 C1
Shelton Gdns. SY1 34 A1
Shelton La. SY3 34 C1
Shelton Pk. SY3 34 C1
Shelton Rd. SY3 34 B1
Sherbourne Rd. SY1 34 C1
Shillington Dri. SY1 31 G1
Shomere Cres. SY3 35 D2
Shop Latch. SY1 36 C3
Shorncliffe Dri. SY3 34 C2
Shorncliffe Way. SY3 34 C2

Shrewsbury By-Pass.
  SY1 31 H1
Silkmoor. SY3 36 B1
Silver Birch Dri. SY3 35 B1
Silverstone Clo. SY3 34 A2
Singleton Av. SY3 35 B2
Six Acres. SY3 34 D5
Smithfield Rd. SY1 36 C2
Snowdrop Clo. SY3 32 D5
Somerby Dri. SY3 34 A1
South Clo. SY3 32 B4
South Hermitage. SY3 32 C4
Southgate Dri. SY2 33 G5
Southville Clo. SY3 34 D5
Spa St. SY3 32 D4
Sparkham Clo. SY3 34 C4
Sparrow La. SY2 33 E3
Spinney Path. SY2 33 F1
Spring Gdns. SY1 30 D6
Springfield Grn. SY2 33 F5
Springfield Way. SY2 33 F5
Springmere. SY3 35 C6
Stanhill Rd. SY3 34 D5
Stanley La. SY3 35 B1
Stanton Grn. SY1 31 G3
Stapleton Rd. SY3 35 D2
Starcross Clo. SY3 34 B1
Station Rd. SY3 35 C1
Steepside. SY3 34 C4
Stephenson Dri. SY2 32 D4
Stersacre. SY1 30 D1
Stilton Clo. SY3 34 C3
Stokesay Av. SY1 30 D3
Stonehurst Dri. SY3 33 E4
Stones Sq. SY3 32 C4
Stretton Clo. SY3 33 E6
Strickland. SY1 30 D2
Sultan Rd. SY1 30 D6
Summers Gdns. SY3 32 C4
Summit Clo. SY3 32 D5
Sundorne Av. SY1 31 F3
Sundorne Cres. SY1 31 F3
Sundorne Rd. SY1 31 E4
Sunfield Gdns. SY3 35 A5
Sunfield Pk. SY3 33 F4
Sunnybank Rd. SY2 33 E5
Sussex Av. SY3 32 C5
Sutton Gro. SY2 33 E5
Sutton La. SY3 32 D4
Sutton La. SY3 32 D6
Sutton Rd. SY2 33 E6
Sutton Way. SY2 33 E5
Swallow Dri. SY1 31 H2
Swan Hill. SY1 36 C3
Sweet Lake. SY3 35 B2
Swift Clo. SY1 31 H2
Swiss Farm Rd. SY1 34 B2
Sydney Av. SY1 31 E6
Talcott Dri. SY3 34 D5
Talisman Dri. SY2 33 F2
Tanfield. SY1 30 C4
Tankerville St. SY2 33 E2
Tansley Clo. SY3 34 C3
Tarvin Rd. SY1 30 D6
Tawnylea. SY1 30 C4
Telford Way. SY1 31 E4
Tenbury Dri. SY3 33 G1
The Bank. SY1 30 D1
The Bradleys. SY1 31 H2
The Broad Well. SY3 34 D5
The Cedars. SY3 33 E3
The Cinder Path. SY3 32 B4
The Common. SY3 34 D5
The Crescent. SY3 36 C3
The Dana. SY1 36 E1
The Hassacks. SY1 31 H3
The Hawthorns. SY3 32 D4
The Hig. SY1 31 H3
The Mall. SY1 36 C2
The Maltings. SY3 35 B5
The Mount. SY3 34 C1
The Parade. SY1 30 D2
The Parks. SY1 31 G2
The Redlands. SY3 33 E4
The Rocks. SY3 32 C5
The Springs. SY1 31 G2
The Square. SY1 36 C3
Thieves La. SY1 33 G6
Thomas Clo. SY3 36 E3
Thornhill Rd. SY1 30 C4
Thornton Rd. SY1 30 C4
Tilbrook Dri. SY1 31 E6
Tilstock Cres. SY3 33 E6
Tindale Clo. SY3 34 B1
Topham Clo. SY3 33 E5
Torrin Rd. SY3 34 D4

Town Walls. SY1 36 C3
Trafalgar Pl. SY2 32 D1
Tresta Clo. SY3 34 D5
Trinity Pl. SY3 36 E4
Trinity St. SY3 32 D4
Tudor Rd. SY2 33 E5
Two Ashes. SY3 35 B5
Twyfords Way. SY3 33 G1
Underdale Av. SY2 33 E1
Underdale Rd. SY2 33 E1
Uplands Dri. SY2 32 D5
Upper Rd. SY3 32 B5
Uppington Av. SY3 32 C4
Upton La. SY3 33 F1
Vane Rd. SY3 32 B4
Vennington Walk. SY2 31 F6
Vicarage Rd. SY3 35 C1
Victoria Av. SY1 36 A2
Victoria Rd. SY3 35 C1
Victoria St. SY1 36 E1
Victoria Ter. SY1 32 D1
Victorian Arcade. SY1 36 C2
Waincott. SY1 30 D1
Walkford Clo. SY3 34 D4
Walnut Dri. SY1 30 D2
Walsham Clo. SY3 34 D5
Walton Rd. SY3 32 D5
Warrenby Clo. SY1 31 E5
Washford Rd. SY3 35 A2
Watchcote. SY1 30 C5
Water St. SY1 32 D1
Waverton Way. SY3 34 B1
Wayford Clo. SY3 35 D2
Wayhill. SY1 30 D1
Weald Dri. SY2 33 G1
Wellbury Clo. SY3 35 C5
Wellington Clo. SY1 31 F4
Wellmeadow Dri. SY3 34 C2
Wellmeadow Gdns.
  SY3 34 C2
Wellmeadow Rd. SY3 34 C2
Wellwood Clo. SY3 34 A2
Welsh Br. SY3 36 B2
Welshpool Rd. SY3 34 A1
Wendsley Rd. SY1 30 D2
Wenlock Rd. SY2 33 E3
Wentworth Clo. SY3 35 A5
West Hermitage. SY3 32 C4
West St. SY1 32 D1
Westbourne Rise. SY3 35 A5
Westbury Rd. SY1 30 D2
Westhope Av. SY3 34 B2
Westlands Rd. SY3 34 B2
Westminster Dri. SY1 30 C6
Westmoreland Mews.
  SY1 30 C6
Weston Dri. SY1 30 D4
Westwood Dri. SY1 34 C1
Weybourne Rd. SY3 34 D5
Wheatley. SY1 31 F4
Whiston Clo. SY3 34 C4
Whitchurch Rd. SY1 31 E4
White Hart. SY3 32 D5
White Meadow Clo.
  SY1 30 C5
Whitecroft Rd. SY3 32 D5
Whitehall Mews. SY2 33 E2
Whitehall St. SY2 32 D1
Whitehorse Pass. SY3 36 B1
Whitehouse Gdns.
  SY1 30 D4
Whitemere Rd. SY3 30 D4
Whittington Clo. SY1 31 H3
Whitton Clo. SY2 33 E6
Wilderley Cres. SY3 35 C3
Wildon Way. SY3 34 B2
Willington Clo. SY3 30 D1
Willow Rd. SY3 34 C1
Willowdale Gdns. SY1 30 C5
Wilton Green. SY3 35 D2
Windermere Rd. SY3 31 E3
Windsor Pl. SY1 30 D2
Wingfield Clo. SY1 30 D5
Wingfield Gdns. SY1 30 D5
Winifred Clo. SY2 33 G3
Winterton Way. SY3 34 A1
Wood St. SY1 30 C6
Wood Sd Gdns. SY1 30 C6
Woodbank Dri. SY3 34 D3
Woodcote Way. SY3 31 F6
Woodfield Av. SY3 34 D2
Woodfield Rd. SY3 32 A2
Woodlands Clo. SY3 30 E3
Woodlands Pk. SY3 33 E3
Woodlark Clo. SY1 31 H3
Woodlea. SY2 33 F5

Woodpecker Clo. SY1 31 H
Woodside Dri. SY3 34 D
Worcester Rd. SY1 30 D
Worthington Dri. SY3 34 C
Wren Ct. SY1 31 H
Wyle Cop. SY1 36 D
Yewtree Clo. SY3 35 B
York Rd. SY1 30 D

TELFORD CENTRE

*Ashdown La, Telford
  Shopping Centre. TF3 37 E
Boyd Clo. TF3 37 E
Church Rd. TF3 37 A
Coach Central. TF3 37 E
Coachwell Clo. TF3 37 A
Colliers Way. TF3 37 A
Dale Acre Way. TF3 37 C
Dalelands. TF3 37 C
Dalford Ct. TF3 37 C
Danesford. TF3 37 C
Dark Lane Dri. TF3 37 A
*Dean Sq, Telford Shopping
  Centre. TF3 37 E
*Dean St, Telford Shopping
  Centre. TF3 37 E
Deepdale. TF3 37 D
Deercote. TF3 37 C
Delbury Ct. TF3 37 C
Dinchope Dri. TF3 37 D
Downemead. TF3 37 D
Downton Ct. TF3 37 D
Draycott. TF3 37 D
Duffryn. TF3 37 D
Dunsheath. TF3 37 C
Dunstone. TF3 37 C
Euston Way. TF3 37 C
Farm Lodge Gro. TF3 37 A
Forgegate. TF3 37 B
Grange Central. TF3 37 C
Hall Park Way. TF3 37 A
Hollinsgate. TF3 37 C
Hollinswood Rd. TF2 37 C
Holyhead Rd. TF2 37 B
INDUSTRIAL & RETAIL:
Castle Trading Est.
  TF3 37 C
Forge Retail Pk. TF3 37 A
Priorslee Trading Est.
  TF2 37 D
Telford Bridge
  Retail Park. TF3 37 A
Telford Shopping
  Centre. TF3 37 B
Ironmasters Way. TF3 37 E
*Kielder Sq, Telford Shopping
  Centre. TF3 37 E
Lawn Central. TF3 37 C
Lawns Wood. TF3 37 C
Malingsate. TF3 37 C
*New Row, Telford Shopping
  Centre. TF3 37 E
*New St, Telford Shopping
  Centre. TF3 37 E
*North Sherwood St, Telford
  Shopping Centre. TF3 37 E
Priorslee Rd. TF2 37 D
Queen Elizabeth Av.
  TF3 37 C
Queensway. TF3 37 C
Queenswood Clo. TF2 37 B
Rampart Way. TF3 37 C
St Quentin Gate. TF3 37 C
*Sherwood Row, Telford
  Shopping Centre. TF3 37 E
*Sherwood Sq, Telford
  Shopping Centre. TF3 37 E
*Sherwood St, Telford
  Shopping Centre. TF3 37 E
Silkin Way. TF3 37 C
Sixth Av. TF2 37 A
*Southwater, Telford
  Shopping Centre. TF3 37 E
*Southwater Arcade, Telford
  Shopping Centre. TF3 37 E
Southwater Way. TF3 37 C
Spout Vw. TF3 37 C
Spout Way. TF3 37 C
Stafford Park Rd. TF3 37 E
Stirchley Av. TF3 37 A
Telford Way. TF3 37 C

he Border, Telford
Shopping Centre. TF3 37 B4
hetford Chase, Telford
Shopping Centre. TF3 37 B4
ird Av. TF2 37 B1
ellswood Av. TF2 37 B1
thywood Dri. TF3 37 A5
oodhouse Central.
TF3 37 B4
Vrekin Sq, Telford Shopping
Centre. TF3 37 B4
Vrekin Wk, Telford
Shopping Centre. TF3 37 B4
tes Way. TF2 37 A1

WELLINGTON

dison Rd. TF1 38 B3
maston Rd. TF1 38 A1
bert Rd. TF1 38 D2
exandra Rd. TF1 38 B3
verley Clo. TF1 38 D2
ley Av. TF1 38 C1
ley Dri. TF1 38 C1
pledore Gdns. TF1 38 C4
ton Clo. TF1 38 D2
as Gro. TF1 38 B3
ondale Rd. TF1 38 A5
gley Dri. TF1 38 B1
rnet Clo. TF1 38 B1
rnfield Ct. TF1 38 B5
rnfield Cres. TF1 38 B5
ech Clo. TF1 38 A2
l St. TF1 38 C3
idden Pl. TF1 38 B1
dge Rd. TF1 38 C2
onte Clo. TF1 38 B2
ldwas Rd. TF1 38 B1
vers Clo. TF1 38 B4
arlton St. TF1 38 C2
estnut Dri. TF1 38 A2
ristine Av. TF1 38 C4
urch Rd. TF1 38 C3
urch Walk. TF1 38 D3
t Cres. TF1 38 B3
n Clo. TF1 38 B1
nbury Rd. TF1 38 B1
emere Dri. TF1 38 B2
lege La. TF1 38 D2
nbermere Dri. TF1 38 B2
nstitution Hill. TF1 38 D2
und Clo. TF1 38 B1
nage Cres. TF1 38 B3
scent Rd. TF1 38 C2
wn St. TF1 38 C3
win Rd. TF1 38 C1
e Clo. TF1 38 C1
er Park Rd. TF1 38 B1
nnerville Clo. TF1 38 A1
nnerville Gdns. TF5 38 A1
pers Ct. TF1 38 C2
ke St. TF1 38 C3
park Dri. TF1 38 A2
all Gdns. TF1 38 C3
all La. TF1 38 B5
ter Dri. TF1 38 D2
field Ct. TF1 38 C2
nstead Ct. TF1 38 A4
wler Clo. TF1 38 C1
orge Pl. TF1 38 B3
be St. TF1 38 D3
f Links La. TF1 38 C5
inger Dri. TF1 38 D1
oms Alley. TF1 38 C3
npton Hill. TF1 38 B5
vington Clo. TF1 38 C1
gate Dri. TF1 38 B4
gate Rd. TF1 38 A4
th Rd. TF1 38 C1
bert Av. TF1 38 B4
tford Clo. TF1 38 D2
ba Clo. TF1 38 B3
Heywood Longsdale Ct.
TF1 38 D3
Hiatt Av. TF1 38 D2
High St. TF1 38 D3
Hollies Rd. TF1 38 B2
Holme Ct. TF1 38 D1
Holyhead Rd. TF1 38 A4
Hordley Rd. TF1 38 B1
Ivy Gro. TF1 38 B3
Jay Dri. TF1 38 D1
King St. TF1 38 C2
Kingfisher Way. TF1 38 D1
Kingshaye Rd. TF1 38 C4
Ladycroft. TF1 38 C2
Lawrence Rd. TF1 38 B3
Lea Ct. TF1 38 D1
Leaton Dri. TF1 38 B1
Leegomery Rd. TF1 38 C2
Lime Tree Way. TF1 38 D1
Limekiln La. TF1 38 D4
Linden Av. TF1 38 B3
Linden Gro. TF1 38 B3
Lindfield Dri. TF1 38 B2
Longford Rise. TF1 38 D1
Longnor Rd. TF1 38 B1
Lowe Ct. TF1 38 D3
Maddocks Ct. TF1 38 D3
Mansell Rd. TF1 38 B3
Market Sq. TF1 38 C3
Market St. TF1 38 C3
Martin Rd. TF1 38 B3
Marton Dri. TF1 38 B1
Meadow Rd. TF1 38 A5
Meese Clo. TF1 38 C1
Melrose Gdns. TF1 38 B3
Merridale Cres. TF1 38 D2
Meyrick Rd. TF1 38 C1
Mill Bank. TF1 38 D3
Montgomery Rd. TF1 38 B3
Nelson Ct. TF1 38 D3
Nevil Rd. TF1 38 B2
New Church Rd. TF1 38 D4
New Hall Rd. TF1 38 D3
New St. TF1 38 C3
Newtonmere Dri. TF1 38 B2
North Rd. TF1 38 B2
Oaks Cres. TF1 38 A5
Oliver Ct. TF1 38 D2
Onslow Dri. TF1 38 B1
Orleton La. TF1 38 B2
Paddock Clo. TF1 38 B2
Park St. TF1 38 C2
Parklands. TF1 38 C1
Parklands Rd. TF1 38 C1
Pembroke Dri. TF1 38 D2
Pendil Clo. TF1 38 A4
Perry Ct. TF1 38 C1
Plough Rd. TF1 38 C2
Poplar Dri. TF1 38 B2
Powder La. TF1 38 B3
Powis Dri. TF1 38 B2
Princes St. TF1 38 D4
Priory Ct. TF1 38 D4
Prospect Rd. TF1 38 D3
Queen St. TF1 38 C2
Rea Dri. TF1 38 B1
Regent St. TF1 38 D3
Richmond Ct. TF1 38 C1
Roden Clo. TF1 38 C1
Rose Cres. TF1 38 C4
Rose Gro. TF1 38 D4
Roseway. TF1 38 C3
Roslyn Rd. TF1 38 D2
Rosthwaite. TF1 38 D4
Rowton Clo. TF1 38 D1
Rushbury Rd. TF1 38 B1
St Chads Clo. TF1 38 C1
St John St. TF1 38 D3
St Margarets Dri. TF1 38 D1
School Ct. TF1 38 D3
School La. TF1 38 D4
Severn Dri. TF1 38 B1
Simon Clo. TF1 38 C3
Spring Hill. TF1 38 B2
Stanley Rd. TF1 38 D3
Station Rd. TF1 38 C3
Steventon Rd. TF1 38 B3
Stokesay Rd. TF1 38 B1
Strine Clo. TF1 38 B1
Sutherland Av. TF1 38 D2
Sutherland Rd. TF1 38 D2
Sycamore Clo. TF1 38 A2
Tan Bank. TF1 38 C3
Telford Mews. TF1 38 B5
Telford Rd. TF1 38 B5
Tern Way. TF1 38 C1
The Lawns. TF1 38 C2
The Parade. TF1 38 C3
Union Rd. TF1 38 C4
Victoria Av. TF1 38 D3
Victoria Rd. TF1 38 C3
Victoria St. TF1 38 D3
Vineyard Dri. TF1 38 C2
Vineyard Pl. TF1 38 B2
Vineyard Rd. TF1 38 C2
Walker St. TF1 38 C3
Waterloo Rd. TF1 38 D3
Wellington Rd. TF5 38 A1
West Rd. TF1 38 B3
Weston Dri. TF1 38 B2
Weyman Rd. TF1 38 B1
Whitchurch Dri. TF1 38 D1
Whitchurch Rd. TF1 38 C1
Whitemere Rd. TF1 38 B2
Woodlands Av. TF1 38 B3
Wrekin Rd. TF1 38 C3
Wrockwardine Rd. TF1 38 A2
Wyke Rise. TF1 38 D1

WEM

Arden Clo. SY4 39 D1
Ash Gro. SY4 39 D1
Aston Rd. SY4 39 C2
Aston St. SY4 39 B2
Bailey Clo. SY4 39 A1
Bank House La. SY4 39 A3
Barleyfields. SY4 39 C1
Barnard St. SY4 39 B2
Barnfield Av. SY4 39 B1
Blacon Clo. SY4 39 B4
Bowenfields. SY4 39 B1
Brook Dri. SY4 39 B3
Butler Rd. SY4 39 B1
Castle Ct. SY4 39 B2
Cedar Clo. SY4 39 B2
Cedar Gro. SY4 39 B1
Chapel St. SY4 39 B2
Church La. SY4 39 D2
Churchill Dri. SY4 39 D2
Cordwell Pl. SY4 39 C2
Crabtree La. SY4 39 B1
Crown St. SY4 39 B2
Davies Rd. SY4 39 B1
Drawwell La. SY4 39 B3
Drawwell Walk. SY4 39 B1
Ekford Pk. SY4 39 B3
Ellesmere Rd. SY4 39 A2
Fothergill Way. SY4 39 A3
Foxleigh Clo. SY4 39 C1
Foxleigh Cres. SY4 39 C1
Foxleigh Dri. SY4 39 C1
Foxleigh Grn. SY4 39 C1
Garbett Clo. SY4 39 B2
Greenacres. SY4 39 C1
Harris Croft. SY4 39 C2
Hawkstone Dri. SY4 39 D2
Hazlitt Pl. SY4 39 C2
High St. SY4 39 B2
Hough La. SY4 39 B3
INDUSTRIAL & RETAIL:
Wem Business Park.
SY4 39 B2
Kynaston Dri. SY4 39 C1
Lacon Dri. SY4 39 D2
Leek St. SY4 39 B2
Lowe Hill Gdns. SY4 39 A1
Lowe Hill Rd. SY4 39 A1
Market St. SY4 39 B2
Marlcroft. SY4 39 B1
Meadow Clo. SY4 39 B1
Mill St. SY4 39 B3
New St. SY4 39 B2
Noble St. SY4 39 B2
Orchard Way. SY4 39 C2
Pantulf Rd. SY4 39 C1
Park Rd. SY4 39 C2
Prince William Ct. SY4 39 C2
Pyms Rd. SY4 39 A1
Queensway. SY4 39 C1
Ranford Way. SY4 39 C1
Roden Gro. SY4 39 B3
Roden Lodge. SY4 39 B3
Shrubbery Gdns. SY4 39 C1
Somerset Way. SY4 39 A1
Soulton Cres. SY4 39 D2
Soulton Rd. SY4 39 C2
Station Rd. SY4 39 C1
Summerfield. SY4 39 C1
Sungrove. SY4 39 B3
Tannery Ct. SY4 39 B2
The Grove. SY4 39 B2
Three Gates. SY4 39 D2
Tilley Rd. SY4 39 B3
Trentham Clo. SY4 39 B1
Trentham Rd. SY4 39 B1
Weir La. SY4 39 D3
Wellgate. SY4 39 B3
Wemsbrook Dri. SY4 39 B1
Wemsbrook Rd. SY4 39 B1

WHITCHURCH

Alkington Gdns. SY13 39 B6
Alkington Rd. SY13 39 B6
Alport Rd. SY13 39 C4
Anchor Clo. SY13 39 D5
Bargates. SY13 39 B4
Bark Hill. SY13 39 C5
Barnfield Clo. SY13 39 A4
Bath St. SY13 39 D4
Bathfields Cres. SY13 39 A5
Beatrice Gdns. SY13 39 D4
Belton Clo. SY13 39 A5
Belton Rd. SY13 39 A6
Black Park Rd. SY13 39 D4
Blackmore Gro. SY13 39 C4
Blakemere Clo. SY13 39 C4
Bridgewater St. SY13 39 C5
Brook Rd. SY13 39 C5
Brookfield. SY13 39 A5
Brownlow St. SY13 39 C4
Bryn Estynay. SY13 39 B4
Bull Ring. SY13 39 C5
Burway Dri. SY13 39 D5
Caldecott Cres. SY13 39 A5
Castillion Dri. SY13 39 D4
Castle Ct. SY13 39 B4
Castle Hill. SY13 39 C5
Chemistry. SY13 39 A5
Chester Av. SY13 39 A4
Chester Rd. SY13 39 A4
Chorton Dri. SY13 39 D5
Church Meadows.
SY13 39 C4
Church St. SY13 39 C4
Church View. SY13 39 C5
Claypit St. SY13 39 C4
Clayton Dri. SY13 39 C4
De Warenne Clo. SY13 39 D6
Deep Moss. SY13 39 C5
Dodington. SY13 39 C5
Dodington Clo. SY13 39 C5
Edgeley Rd. SY13 39 C6
Edward German Dri.
SY13 39 C5
*Egerton Ct,
Egerton Rd. SY13 39 D4
Egerton Pl. SY13 39 C4
Egerton Rd. SY13 39 D4
Elizabeth St. SY13 39 D4
Fraser Ct. SY13 39 C6
George St. SY13 39 D4
Green End. SY13 39 C5
*Green End Par,
Deep Moss. SY13 39 C5
Greenfields Way. SY13 39 A4
Haroldgate. SY13 39 B4
Heronbrook. SY13 39 A4
High St. SY13 39 C4
Highfields Av. SY13 39 B6
Highgate. SY13 39 B5
Hillewood Av. SY13 39 B6
Kent Clo. SY13 39 D6
Kingsway. SY13 39 C6
Kingsway Ct. SY13 39 C6
Linden Av. SY13 39 B5
Liverpool Rd. SY13 39 B6
London Rd. SY13 39 C4
Meadow Croft. SY13 39 A5
Meadow View Rd.
SY13 39 B5
*Melton Mews,
Victoria Clo. SY13 39 C5
Mill St. SY13 39 C5
*Nelson Ter,
Egerton Rd. SY13 39 D4
Neufchatel Clo. SY13 39 D5
Neufchatel Ct. SY13 39 D5
Newport Rd. SY13 39 C5
Newtown. SY13 39 B5
Oak Dri. SY13 39 B6
Osmere Clo. SY13 39 C4
Park Av. SY13 39 C5
Park Rd. SY13 39 B5
Pauls Moss. SY13 39 C6
Pauls Moss Ct. SY13 39 C6
Pear Tree La. SY13 39 A4
Pearl Yd. SY13 39 C5
Pepper St. SY13 39 C5
Prees Rd. SY13 39 D6
Queens Rd. SY13 39 D5
Queensway. SY13 39 C6
Roman Way. SY13 39 B4
Rosemary La. SY13 39 C5
Rydal Av. SY13 39 D6
Sadlers Walk. SY13 39 B6
St Alkmunds Mdw.
SY13 39 B4
St Johns St. SY13 39 C4
St Marys St. SY13 39 C4
Salisbury Rd. SY13 39 D5
Scotland St. SY13 39 B5
Sedgeford. SY13 39 C6
Sharps Dri. SY13 39 A5
Sherrymill Hill. SY13 39 B5
Smallbrook Bldgs.
SY13 39 B4
Smallbrook Rd. SY13 39 A5
Stags Leap. SY13 39 A4
Station Rd. SY13 39 D5
Talbot Cres. SY13 39 D5
Talbot St. SY13 39 D5
Tarporley Rd. SY13 39 B4
The Firs. SY13 39 B4
The Wharfage. SY13 39 C5
Thompson Dri. SY13 39 A5
Tilstock Rd. SY13 39 C6
Victoria Clo. SY13 39 C5
Walnut Dri. SY13 39 B6
Watergate. SY13 39 C5
Waterside Clo. SY13 39 B4
Waylands Av. SY13 39 D6
Waylands Clo. SY13 39 D6
Waymills. SY13 39 D5
Wellfield Way. SY13 39 B4
Westbrook Av. SY13 39 A5
Weston Court Mews.
SY13 39 C5
Westune Clo. SY13 39 B6
Whitchurch By-Pass.
SY13 39 A5
Worthington St. SY13 39 D4
Wrexham Rd. SY13 39 A5
Yardington. SY13 39 B4

Edition 211 H 05.01.

ESTATE PUBLICATIONS

RED BOOKS

ALDERSHOT, CAMBERLEY
ALFRETON, BELPER, RIPLEY
ASHFORD, TENTERDEN
BANGOR, CAERNARFON
BARNSTAPLE, ILFRACOMBE
BASILDON, BILLERICAY
BASINGSTOKE, ANDOVER
BATH, BRADFORD-ON-AVON
BEDFORD
BIRMINGHAM, WOLVERHAMPTON, COVENTRY
BOURNEMOUTH, POOLE, CHRISTCHURCH
BRACKNELL
BRENTWOOD
BRIGHTON, LEWES, NEWHAVEN, SEAFORD
BRISTOL
BROMLEY (London Bromley)
BURTON-UPON-TRENT, SWADLINCOTE
BURY ST. EDMUNDS
CAMBRIDGE
CARDIFF
CARLISLE
CHELMSFORD, BRAINTREE, MALDON, WITHAM
CHESTER
CHESTERFIELD
CHICHESTER, BOGNOR REGIS
COLCHESTER, CLACTON
CORBY, KETTERING
CRAWLEY & MID SUSSEX
CREWE
DERBY, HEANOR, CASTLE DONINGTON
EASTBOURNE, BEXHILL, SEAFORD, NEWHAVEN
EDINBURGH, MUSSELBURGH, PENICUIK
EXETER, EXMOUTH
FALKIRK, GRANGEMOUTH
FAREHAM, GOSPORT
FLINTSHIRE TOWNS
FOLKESTONE, DOVER, DEAL & ROMNEY MARSH
GLASGOW, & PAISLEY
GLOUCESTER, CHELTENHAM
GRAVESEND, DARTFORD
GRAYS, THURROCK
GREAT YARMOUTH, LOWESTOFT
GRIMSBY, CLEETHORPES
GUILDFORD, WOKING
HARLOW, BISHOPS STORTFORD
HASTINGS, BEXHILL, RYE
HEREFORD
HERTFORD, HODDESDON, WARE
HIGH WYCOMBE
HUNTINGDON, ST. NEOTS
IPSWICH, FELIXSTOWE
ISLE OF MAN
ISLE OF WIGHT TOWNS
KENDAL
KIDDERMINSTER
KINGSTON-UPON-HULL
LANCASTER, MORECAMBE
LEICESTER, LOUGHBOROUGH
LINCOLN
LLANDUDNO, COLWYN BAY
LUTON, DUNSTABLE
MACCLESFIELD
MAIDSTONE
MANSFIELD, MANSFIELD WOODHOUSE
MEDWAY, GILLINGHAM
MILTON KEYNES
NEW FOREST TOWNS
NEWPORT, CHEPSTOW
NEWTOWN, WELSHPOOL
NORTHAMPTON
NORTHWICH, WINSFORD
NORWICH
NOTTINGHAM, EASTWOOD, HUCKNALL, ILKESTON
OXFORD, ABINGDON
PENZANCE, ST. IVES
PETERBOROUGH
PLYMOUTH, IVYBRIDGE, SALTASH, TORPOINT
PORTSMOUTH, HAVANT, WATERLOOVILLE
READING
REDDITCH, BROMSGROVE
REIGATE, BANSTEAD, LEATHERHEAD, DORKING

RHYL, PRESTATYN
RUGBY
ST. ALBANS, WELWYN, HATFIELD
SALISBURY, AMESBURY, WILTON
SCUNTHORPE
SEVENOAKS
SHREWSBURY
SITTINGBOURNE, FAVERSHAM, ISLE OF SHEPPEY
SLOUGH, MAIDENHEAD, WINDSOR
SOUTHAMPTON, EASTLEIGH
SOUTHEND-ON-SEA
STAFFORD
STEVENAGE, HITCHIN, LETCHWORTH
STIRLING
STOKE-ON-TRENT
STROUD, NAILSWORTH
SWANSEA, NEATH, PORT TALBOT
SWINDON, CHIPPENHAM, MARLBOROUGH
TAUNTON, BRIDGWATER
TELFORD
THANET, CANTERBURY, HERNE BAY, WHITSTABLE
TORBAY (Torquay, Paignton, Newton Abbot)
TRURO, FALMOUTH
TUNBRIDGE WELLS, TONBRIDGE, CROWBOROUGH
WARWICK, ROYAL LEAMINGTON SPA &
      STRATFORD UPON AVON
WATFORD, HEMEL HEMPSTEAD
WELLINGBOROUGH
WESTON-SUPER-MARE, CLEVEDON
WEYMOUTH, DORCHESTER
WINCHESTER, NEW ARLESFORD
WORCESTER, DROITWICH
WORTHING, LITTLEHAMPTON, ARUNDEL
WREXHAM
YORK

COUNTY RED BOOKS (Town Centre Maps)

BEDFORDSHIRE
BERKSHIRE
BUCKINGHAMSHIRE
CAMBRIDGESHIRE
CHESHIRE
CORNWALL
DERBYSHIRE
DEVON
DORSET
ESSEX
GLOUCESTERSHIRE
HAMPSHIRE
HEREFORDSHIRE
HERTFORDSHIRE
KENT
LEICESTERSHIRE & RUTLAND
LINCOLNSHIRE
NORFOLK
NORTHAMPTONSHIRE
NOTTINGHAMSHIRE
OXFORDSHIRE
SHROPSHIRE
SOMERSET
STAFFORDSHIRE
SUFFOLK
SURREY
SUSSEX (EAST)
SUSSEX (WEST)
WILTSHIRE
WORCESTERSHIRE

OTHER MAPS

KENT TO CORNWALL (1:460,000)
CHINA (1:6,000,000)
INDIA (1:3,750,000)
INDONESIA (1:4,000,000)
NEPAL (1,800,000)
SOUTH EAST ASIA (1:6,000,000)
THAILAND (1:1,600,000)

STREET PLANS

EDINBURGH TOURIST PLAN
ST. ALBANS

OFFICIAL TOURIST & LEISURE MAPS

SOUTH EAST ENGLAND (1:200,000)
KENT & EAST SUSSEX (1:150,000)
SUSSEX & SURREY (1:150,000)
SUSSEX (1:50,000)
SOUTHERN ENGLAND (1:200,000)
ISLE OF WIGHT (1:50,000)
WESSEX (1:200,000)
DORSET (1:50,000)
DEVON & CORNWALL (1:200,000)
CORNWALL (1:180,000)
DEVON (1:200,000)
DARTMOOR & SOUTH DEVON COAST (1:100,000)
EXMOOR & NORTH DEVON COAST (1:100,000)
GREATER LONDON M25 (1:80,000)
EAST ANGLIA (1:200,000)
CHILTERNS & THAMES VALLEY (1:200,000)
THE COTSWOLDS (1:110,000)
COTSWOLDS & SEVERN VALLEY (1:200,000)
WALES (1:250,000)
CYMRU (1:250,000)
THE SHIRES OF MIDDLE ENGLAND (1:250,000)
THE MID SHIRES (Staffs, Shrops, etc.) (1:200,000)
PEAK DISTRICT (1:100,000)
SNOWDONIA (1:125,000)
YORKSHIRE (1:200,000)
YORKSHIRE DALES (1:125,000)
NORTH YORKSHIRE MOORS (1:125,000)
NORTH WEST ENGLAND (1:200,000)
ISLE OF MAN (1:60,000)
NORTH PENNINES & LAKES (1:200,000)
LAKE DISTRICT (1:75,000)
BORDERS OF ENGLAND & SCOTLAND (1:200,000)
BURNS COUNTRY (1:200,000)
HEART OF SCOTLAND (1:200,000)
GREATER GLASGOW (1:150,000)
EDINBURGH & THE LOTHIANS (1:150,000)
ISLE OF ARRAN (1:63,360)
FIFE (1:100,000)
LOCH LOMOND & TROSSACHS (1:150,000)
ARGYLL THE ISLES & LOCH LOMOND (1:275,000)
PERTHSHIRE, DUNDEE & ANGUS (1:150,000)
FORT WILLIAM, BEN NEVIS, GLEN COE (1:185,000)
IONA (1:10,000) & MULL (1:115,000)
GRAMPIAN HIGHLANDS (1:185,000)
LOCH NESS & INVERNESS (1:150,000)
AVIEMORE & SPEY VALLEY (1:150,000)
SKYE & LOCHALSH (1:130,000)
ARGYLL & THE ISLES (1:200,000)
CAITHNESS & SUTHERLAND (1:185,000)
HIGHLANDS OF SCOTLAND (1:275,000)
WESTERN ISLES (1:125,000)
ORKNEY & SHETLAND (1:128,000)
ENGLAND & WALES (1:650,000)
SCOTLAND (1:500,000)
HISTORIC SCOTLAND (1:500,000)
SCOTLAND CLAN MAP (1:625,000)
BRITISH ISLES (1:1,100,000)
GREAT BRITAIN (1:1,100,000)

EUROPEAN LEISURE MAPS

EUROPE (1:3,100,000)
BENELUX (1:600,000)
FRANCE (1:1,000,000)
GERMANY (1:1,000,000
IRELAND (1:625,000)
ITALY (1:1,000,000)
SPAIN & PORTUGAL (1,1,000,000)
CROSS CHANNEL VISITORS' MAP (1:530,000)
WORLD (1:35,000,000)
WORLD FLAT

TOWNS IN NORTHERN FRANCE STREET ATLAS
BOULOGNE SHOPPERS MAP
CALAIS SHOPPERS MAP
DIEPPE SHOPPERS MAP

ESTATE PUBLICATIONS are also
Distributors in the UK for:

INTERNATIONAL TRAVEL MAPS, Canada
HALLWAG, Switzerland
ORDNANCE SURVEY

Catalogue and prices from:
ESTATE PUBLICATIONS
Bridewell House, Tenterden, Kent. TN30 6EP.
Tel: 01580 764225   Fax: 01580 763720
www.estate-publications.co.uk